BREAK
LOOSE

BREAK LOOSE

GEORGE BLOOMER

WHITAKER
HOUSE

BREAK LOOSE:
Find Freedom from Toxic Traps and Spiritual Bondage

Bishop George Bloomer
www.bishopbloomer.com

ISBN: 978-1-62911-827-7
eBook ISBN: 978-1-62911-828-4
Printed in the United States of America
© 2017 by George Bloomer

Whitaker House
1030 Hunt Valley Circle
New Kensington, PA 15068
www.whitakerhouse.com

Library of Congress Cataloging-in-Publication Data

Names: Bloomer, George G., 1963– author.
Title: Break loose : find freedom from toxic traps and spiritual bondage / George G. Bloomer.
Description: New Kensington, PA : Whitaker House, 2017.
Identifiers: LCCN 2017002280 (print) | LCCN 2017010060 (ebook) | ISBN 9781629118277 (trade pbk. : alk. paper) | ISBN 9781629118284 ()
Subjects: LCSH: Liberty—Religious aspects—Christianity. | Spiritual warfare. | Spiritual healing. | Religious addiction—Christianity. | Religious fanaticism—Christianity.
Classification: LCC BT810.3 .B56 2017 (print) | LCC BT810.3 (ebook) | DDC 248.8/6—dc23
LC record available at https://lccn.loc.gov/2017002280

2 3 4 5 6 7 8 9 10 11 12 13 ⊔⊔ 25 24 23 22 21 20 19 18 17

CONTENTS

FOREWORD

The strongest prisons are not those made of concrete and steel, and the worst judgments are never those handed down from a courtroom judge. The most impenetrable fortresses are those constructed by forces such as poverty, sickness and sin. And the most damaging judgments are fear, false accusations, inaccurate perceptions, unfortunate assumptions, a victim mentality, a sense of shame, hopelessness, and many other like conditions.

Jesus saw all of us in our captivity, and came to set us free. In Luke 4:18–19, He said, *"The Spirit of the LORD is upon Me, because He has anointed Me to preach the gospel to the poor; He has sent Me to heal the brokenhearted, to proclaim liberty to the captives and recovery of sight to the blind, to set at liberty those who are oppressed; to preach the acceptable year of the LORD."*

God did not leave us in our pitiful state. He came to give us the glorious liberty that the blood of Christ purchased, and that rightfully belongs to the sons and daughters of God. We now have a heavenly habitation as well as an earthly home.

In Ephesians 2:6, it says, "[He] *raised us up together and made us sit together in the heavenly places in Christ Jesus....*" As believers, we understand that we have been granted citizenship in the kingdom of heaven even while we remain here on the earth. But what makes these words even more inspiring is realizing that the apostle Paul wrote them while he was in chains in a Roman prison.

Anyone can sing a tune on a clear day at noon. I want to hear from someone who can talk about being seated in heavenly places when the sludge of a Roman sewer is swirling around their feet.

My friend, Bishop George Bloomer, knows what it is like to be trapped, or *stuck*, in hopelessness and despair. But he also knows the redemptive power of a resurrected Christ to lift up, to restore, and to redeem. His writing does not employ gauzy symbolism or theoretical platitudes. From the crucible of his own life experience, and from the pages of the Word of God, he provides timeless principles that will not only produce freedom, but perpetuate it.

—*Dr. Rod Parsley*
Founder and senior pastor, World Harvest Church
New York Times best-selling author
Founder, Breakthrough Ministries

INTRODUCTION:
HOW DID YOU GET STUCK?

I used to live up north, where winter snowfalls were frequent and plentiful. After a storm, I often saw cars in a ditch or spinning their wheels alongside a road, going nowhere. *How did they manage to get stuck like that?* I wondered to myself.

Later in my life, I became a pastor, and I soon encountered scenarios that were oddly similar. In my own congregation and everywhere else I preached, I met people who were *stuck* in one way or another. They were spinning their wheels, exerting a considerable amount of energy, but going nowhere in their spiritual lives.

Many Christians have become trapped by addictions. Like a prisoner hauling around a ball and chain, these folks are bound up in drugs, alcohol, cigarettes, sexual perversion, gambling, or the occult.

Other addictions are more subtle. I've found that many people are trapped by debt, hopelessly stuck in their finances. Others seem powerless to improve their health or heal their emotions. And countless people are stuck in toxic relationships that they don't know how to escape.

If you pause right now to look at your own life, what do you see? Are you free to wholeheartedly pursue God's best for you? Or do you find that something is holding you back? Is there some visible or invisible ball and chain hindering you from your full potential?

There are a variety of ways you may have started down the road to spiritual bondage. Perhaps you dabbled in Ouija boards or other occult practices you thought were harmless fun. Maybe you opened the door to oppression through commonly accepted activities like yoga. Perhaps you developed unhealthy soul ties through an immoral relationship. Or maybe you embarked on the slippery slope of drug addiction through smoking weed with your friends.

The good news is that no matter *how* you got stuck, Jesus Christ is the *Liberator*. He, and He alone, offers the keys to your prison. And when He sets you free, you will be free indeed! (See John 8:36.)

If you desire a greater measure of spiritual freedom in Christ, this book is for you!

I've dealt with some of above things myself, and fortunately I've lived to tell about it. Thank God, He has set me free. And best of all, He has given me powerful keys to share with others who want to find that same freedom.

So are you ready to journey to freedom, my friend? Today could be your day to take the first step out of your chains and into the glorious liberty God has called you to!

ONE

A WOMAN WHO GOT SET FREE

One Sabbath day, Jesus was teaching in the synagogue, and *"a woman was there who had been crippled by a spirit for eighteen years"* (Luke 13:11 NIV). Can you imagine how hopeless this woman must have felt? For eighteen long years, she had endured this debilitating condition.

PERHAPS *you* are struggling with some issue in your life today that has persisted for a long time. You feel as though you've tried everything, but to no avail. Like the woman in this story, you still find yourself *"crippled"* by something outside of your control.

It's no fun being spiritually crippled, but it's something we've all experienced. Sometimes it's a medical condition the doctors can't remedy. At other times, it's the bills that come in faster than the income. And many of us at one time or another have found ourselves stuck in an unhealthy relationship we seem powerless to change.

Thankfully, the Bible says, *"With God all things are possible"* (Matthew 19:26). Even when you're unable to help yourself and no human has a solution to your problem, God can break through your troubling circumstances and set you free!

The story goes on to say that this woman *"was bent over and could not straighten up at all"* (Luke 13:11 NIV). This is such an apt picture of what it's like to be burdened down with sin, sickness, or other situations that seem overwhelming. Sometimes the cares of life are simply too much for us to handle, and all we can do is cast our burdens on the Lord. (See Psalm 55:22.)

Notice that the woman was unable to straighten up "*at all.*" Sometimes we still have hopes that we can straighten things out by our own strength and ingenuity. But this woman had come to the end of her own devices. She needed a *miracle*—something only God could do!

Despite her years of suffering, everything was about to change for her in mere moments. Luke 13:12 says "*Jesus saw her*" and "*called her forward.*" Friend, I don't know what you are going through today. But I *do* know this: Jesus sees you. He cares about you. And He is calling you forward to draw near to Him and receive His healing touch.

After eighteen years of suffering, this distressed woman heard Jesus tell her, "*Woman, you are set free from your infirmity*" (verse 12 NIV). The Greek word for *infirmity* is "astheneia," which means to be feeble or have a lack of strength.

Perhaps you can relate!

That's because the Bible teaches we all were "*without strength*" when living in sin. However, though we were powerless to save ourselves, Jesus demonstrated His love and rescued us. (See Romans 5:6–10.) And just as He forgave us and rescued us from sin at our conversion, He's ready to deliver us *today* from whatever situation is still hindering us from our destiny as believers.

How long does it take to be set free? It doesn't have to take long at all! In this story in Luke 13, Jesus "*put his hands on her, and **immediately** she straightened up and praised God*" (verse 13 NIV).

Isn't that beautiful? Can you imagine the joy and amazement she felt? After being bound for eighteen years, this woman received an *instantaneous* deliverance when Jesus touched her. He straightened up her life in a mere moment, just as He can do for you and me when we come to Him in faith.

Friend, you may have endured some illness, addiction, financial lack, or other problems. Perhaps even for years! But remember: Jesus specializes in miraculous turnarounds. He is speaking His Word to you and reaching out His hand to give you the breakthrough you need. This may be your moment to rise up and praise God for loosing you from your infirmity!

One final note is very important here. Jesus didn't attribute this woman's crippled condition to natural causes. He said, *"This dear woman...has been **held in bondage by Satan** for eighteen years. Isn't it right that she be released...?"* (verse 16 NLT).

You see, much of the distress we experience in this life is the result of spiritual warfare and attacks from the enemy. In order to be set free in such cases, we must address the root cause and overcome the devil.

The good news is that you can be assured of victory when you follow God's simple instructions: *"Submit to God. Resist the devil and he will flee from you"* (James 4:7). The Mighty One living in you is far greater than any attack against you. (See 1 John 4:4.)

Before we go any further, I encourage you to pause and insert your *own* name in this powerful statement Jesus made to the crippled woman: "_____, you are set free from your infirmity." As you allow those words to sink deep into your heart, faith will rise and troubles that have persisted for years will melt away quicker than you can imagine!

TWO

TAKE OFF YOUR GRAVECLOTHES

Does it ever seem like the Lord shows up *late* to solve your problems? Well, that's exactly how the disciples felt in John 11. Jesus was called to the bedside of his dying friend, Lazarus. Instead of rushing to the scene, Jesus delayed—and Lazarus died!

Well, don't despair. There's a happy ending to this story, just as the Lord wants to bring happy endings to the difficult situations *you* face today.

We're specifically told in this story that Jesus loved Lazarus. (See verse 5.) So why didn't He save him from death? The simple answer is that Jesus wanted to do a bigger miracle than merely providing a healing. He wanted to perform a *resurrection!* And all this was so that *"the Son of God may be glorified through it"* (verse 4).

Although I don't know what you may be going through today, I'm confident that the resurrection power of God can solve it! And when the supernatural breakthrough comes, He will get all the glory for setting you free.

When Jesus finally arrived at Lazarus' home in Bethany, Lazarus had already been dead and buried for several days. As you can imagine, the family members blamed Jesus for not coming sooner. *"Lord, if You had been here, my brother would not have died,"* Lazarus' sister Martha complained (verse 21).

Present-Tense Faith

Martha's conclusion was quite logical, of course. But it was focused on the *past* instead of the *present*, and on *regrets* instead of *anticipation*.

Perhaps you're feeling like Martha today, with many regrets about failures or missed opportunities in your past. From her perspective, it was simply too late for a miracle. Her brother had died, and she assumed that was the end of the story.

Even when Jesus told Martha that Lazarus would rise again (verse 23), she thought He was talking about some future day of resurrection, *"at the last day"* (verse 24). Yes, this dear woman had plenty of faith that Jesus could have done a miracle in the *past*, if only He had arrived sooner. And she also had lots of faith about the *future* resurrection, many years from then.

But, my friend, Jesus wants to do miracles *today*, in the *present*. Our Lord is *"the same yesterday, today, and forever"* (Hebrews 13:8), so today can be the day He touches your body, finances, family, or emotions with His resurrection power.

A little later in the story, Jesus asked, *"Did I not say to you that if you would believe you would see the glory of God?"* (John 11:40). Notice that faith is a *present-tense* experience that leads to present and future benefits. That's why the Bible says, **"Now faith is the substance of things hoped for, the evidence of things not seen"** (Hebrews 11:1).

Take a second right now to ask yourself whether you have present-tense faith. Or are you so caught up with the experiences of your past or the expectations of your future that you're missing out on the *"now faith"* God wants you to have?

Fortunately, Jesus didn't give up on a miracle for His deceased friend. Nor did He resign Himself to only providing a resurrection for Lazarus on some day in the distant future. He made a move right then and there.

Removing Obstacles

Jesus approached the tomb, which we're told was a cave, blocked by a massive stone. Picture the scene when the Son of God ordered the bewildered onlookers, *"Take away the stone"* (John 11:39).

I love this part of the story, because we all have boulders and obstacles that seem to be standing in the way of the miracle we need from God. It doesn't seem possible for the Lord to even see our situation, let alone remedy it.

And in the case of Lazarus, there was another major problem. *"Lord, by this time there is a stench, for he has been dead four days,"* Martha informed Jesus (verse 39).

What an appropriate picture of the difficult situations we face today! Not only is there a huge stone blocking any hope of breakthrough, but the distressing circumstances have gone on for so long, there's a major odor involved!

This should offer great encouragement as you deal with stinky situations in your life. You would think the spotless Savior would want to *avoid* such an odor, but He never does. As long as we're willing to remove the stone and give Him access, He will take care of the rest.

The climax of John 11 is Jesus crying out with a loud voice, *"Lazarus, come forth!"* (verse 43). Wouldn't you like to have been there to witness this powerful encounter between the Lord of life and the stench of death and decay?

Well, Jesus is saying these same words to you today, my friend. You can come back to life and exit your tomb. You can come out of the dark cave you've been locked in, and you can walk outside into the bright sunshine of a brand-new day.

There was still another step in setting Lazarus free, and it's a crucial part in giving *us* true liberty as well. Although Lazarus miraculously came back to life at Jesus' command, he *"came out bound hand and foot with graveclothes, and his face was wrapped with a cloth"* (verse 44).

This explains so much about why some people get saved, but struggle to find freedom from addictions, fears, and strongholds that were part of their lives before meeting Christ. Yes, they've been raised from death to life, but they've allowed some aspects of their former life to follow them.

Thankfully, Jesus wasn't satisfied with raising His friend back to life, only to have him walk around bound like a mummy! *"Loose him, and let him go,"* Jesus told the bystanders (verse 44).

You see, the job isn't completed at your conversion. There are often stinky graveclothes that impede your growth and progress until you are *loosed* and *set free*.

Before we move on, I want you to be brutally honest with yourself. Are there still some remnants of your past life that are clinging to you like a stinky old garment? Jesus wants unwrap you from them and set you free. What are you waiting for?

THREE

GET OUT OF THE MIRY CLAY

When you meet some folks, they can't stop talking about how rough they've had it in life. Like a bad country ballad from Nashville, they're always singing that "Somebody done me wrong."

Whenever I encounter people who have this "woe is me" mentality, I want to tell them, "Well, join the club, brother! Welcome to the human race!"

You see, we've *all* gone through some stuff, and we'll all go through some more stuff at some point in the future. While we might envy others who seem to have an easy, carefree life, usually that image is only an illusion. No matter what side of town people grow up on, or how rich they may be, storms come to *everyone's* life from time to time.

I could write entire books about the hard times I experienced as a kid. I grew up in deep poverty, living in a government-subsidized housing project in Brooklyn, New York. It was a tough place to live, and my early education was a joke. I went to school each day to get the free breakfast and lunch, and then left to smoke cigarettes or pot with my friends. I finally found myself in high school and unable to read—and I'm embarrassed to admit that I *still* couldn't read until I reached my mid-thirties.

Perhaps you can't relate to these experiences. In fact, I *hope* you can't relate. I know the ghetto is a strange place to grow up. It is filled with hopelessness and despair. Blacks, whites, Latinos, and other ethnicities are locked behind fences of government entitlement, with little hope of breaking out of the prison.

My mother raised my sister and me on welfare, and I saw first-hand how difficult it is to break free from that kind of culture. My sister, and now even her daughter, are still locked in the entitlement trap—the deadly myth that someone owes you something you don't have to work for.

The good news is that none of us are automatically *stuck* with the kind of situation we've inherited. It may be more difficult to break free if life has dealt you a difficult hand, but there's no pit so deep that God can't get you out.

And be clear on this: It's not just terrible sinners who get stuck. Even godly people like King David find themselves on their knees, crying out to God for deliverance:

> I waited patiently for the LORD;
> And He inclined to me,
> And heard my cry.
> He also brought me up out of a horrible pit,
> Out of the miry clay,
> And set my feet upon a rock,
> And established my steps.
> He has put a new song in my mouth—
> Praise to our God;
> Many will see it and fear,
> And will trust in the LORD.   (Psalm 40:1–3)

Perhaps you've found yourself in *"a horrible pit"* filled with *"miry clay"* because of distressing circumstances in your life. If you have, then be encouraged by how God delivered David from the "pit stop" he faced. David gained stability and freedom when his feet were placed on a solid rock. And instead of the dreary ballad David probably had been singing, the Lord gave him *"a new song"* filled with thanksgiving and praise.

If you can't exactly relate to being stuck in a pit, perhaps *The Message* paraphrase offers a clearer picture: *"He lifted me out of the ditch, pulled me from deep mud."* Isn't it good to know that God can lift you out of the ditch and pull you free from the mud?

Of course, the longer you've been stuck in a situation like that, the harder it usually is to break free. Perhaps a word picture will help you understand why this is true: If you attach a baby elephant to a stake in the ground, it soon learns that it's not strong enough to break free. As the years go by and the elephant grows bigger and bigger, he becomes easily powerful enough to pull the stake out of the ground with one yank of his leg, yet he never does. Why? Because he has been conditioned to think he's not *capable* of it.

How sad! Yet many people who grow up in difficult situations are a lot like the elephant who never breaks loose from the stake that once held him captive. Freedom is now possible, but few are bold enough to break the invisible chains that still bind them.

By God's grace and lots of hard work, I'm happy to report that I broke free from all of that bondage—and you can break free from your "ghetto" experiences as well. From being unable to read even as a young adult, I've now written more than thirty books! Praise God. We truly *can* do all things through Christ who strengthens us. (See Philippians 4:13.)

FOUR

TEAR OFF YOUR SCARLET LETTERS

Too often, people think their dismal past will inevitably keep them from a happy future. They are painfully aware of their past mistakes and negative tendencies, and they wonder if things can ever get any better.

As I mentioned, I wasn't much of a student in high school, but I do know that part of the required reading was Nathaniel Hawthorne's famous novel, *The Scarlet Letter*. Set in seventeenth-century Puritan Boston, the book tells the story of Hester Prynne, who is required to sew the letter "A" on her dress after her adultery is discovered.

Think of what it would be like if this kind of punishment was enforced today. What if everyone who had sex outside of marriage was required to wear a scarlet "A" for adultery or "S" for shame?

How ludicrous is it that although such oppression is certainly not enforced, many of us are still carrying around our scarlet letters! Perhaps it's a scarlet "F" for Failure or Fat, "R" for Rejected, "I" for Inferior, "U" for Unemployed, or "D" for Depressed or Divorced.

You get the picture. Life's scarlet letters can be customized to fit your personal situations. If we're not careful, our negative experience can become our identity.

Yes, many people—even many Christians—are carrying around internal guilt, inferiority, and shame that are not much different than Hester Prynne's cruel punishment. Unable to believe God has truly forgiven them, they still are wallowing in their past mistakes.

I love the gospel of Jesus Christ because it's a message of redemption and happy endings. No matter how you've messed up your life with poor decisions in the past, God can set you free and give you a glorious future.

If you don't believe me, take a look at the story of Rahab, a prostitute living in Jericho. (See Joshua 2.) This woman had a history far worse than Hester Prynne's. She undoubtedly had engaged in sexual relations many men, not just one. Rahab was likely seen as one of Jericho's most notorious home-wreckers.

Yet this Canaanite harlot ends up in the Hall of Fame of Faith in Hebrews 11 and even in the family line of both King David and Jesus. (See Hebrews 11:31 and Matthew 1:5.) What an amazing turnaround!

Despite growing up in a pagan environment, Rahab had heard of the God of Israel, and faith grew in her heart that He was the true God. So when Joshua sent two spies to scout out the fortified city of Jericho, she hid them on her roof and lied to the king's soldiers about the spies' whereabouts.

Quite the opposite of wearing a scarlet letter for her sordid past, Rahab ended up being *saved* by scarlet of a different kind. The spies agreed to spare her life if she hung a scarlet cord from her window so the Israelites could find and protect her after the city fell. (See Joshua 2:17–21.)

Do you see what a beautiful picture this is? The scarlet cord represents the blood of Jesus that later would be shed on the cross for the sins of the world. (See John 1:29.) Like Rahab, *none* of us can stand before God on the basis of our own good deeds or righteousness.

As the old hymn by Robert Lowry says:

What can wash away my sin?
    Nothing but the blood of Jesus;
What can make me whole again?
    Nothing but the blood of Jesus.

O precious is the flow
That makes me white as snow;
No other fount I know;
    Nothing but the blood of Jesus.[1]

---

1. Robert Lowry, "Nothing but the Blood," 1876.

My friend, there's no need for you to keep wearing that scarlet letter of guilt and shame for things you've done in the past. This is a new day for you. When the devil comes to condemn you, you can hang the scarlet cord from your window and tell him the blood of Jesus has cleansed you, just as if you had never sinned.

By taking a step of faith, Rahab changed the whole trajectory of her life. Not only was her own life transformed, but her legacy has now impacted countless generations. I'm believing God for the same kind of transformation to happen in *your* life. So go to God in prayer today and ask Him to show you whether you've been carrying around a "scarlet letter" because of mistakes you've made in the past. If so, claim the promise of Isaiah 1:18 that God can cleanse away your sins and make them *"white as snow."*

Notice that this doesn't say, "After you're forgiven you'll be some shade of *gray!*" No, God will make you *"white as snow,"* just as if you had never sinned. So go ahead and thank Him for the blood of Jesus that makes this possible!

And be clear on this: Your heavenly Father doesn't just tolerate you or begrudgingly accept you. He wholeheartedly *loves* you and offers you an incredible new identity:

> *The LORD will hold you in his hand for all to see—*
> *a splendid crown in the hand of God.*
> *Never again will you be called "The Forsaken City"*
> *Or "The Desolate Land."*
> *Your new name will be "The City of God's Delight"*
> *And "The Bride of God,"*
> *For the LORD delights in you*
> *And will claim you as his bride.*   (Isaiah 62:3–4 NLT)

Amazing love, isn't it? You are *"God's Delight,"* and He beckons you to live your life as His beloved bride. You can throw away your scarlet letters, once and for all.

FIVE

YOUR INVITATION TO A PARTY

Countless books and sermons have been written and preached to give people advice on overcoming drugs, pornography, smoking, alcoholism, codependence, and all sorts of other forms of addiction. And while I'm sure you've probably heard a lot of good information on these issues, I want to share an approach that is quite *different*.

Yes, I want to help you overcome some things. But my focus is more on the positive: instead of telling you what *not* to do, I want to help you find a new level of freedom in Christ, so you can fulfill His highest purposes for your life.

Too often, preachers focus on eradicating people's sins without pointing them to something higher and better. In the long run, this approach always falls flat. Why? Because in order to have lasting victory in our lives, our eyes must be fixed on *Jesus* rather than focused on our failures. (See Hebrews 12:1–2.)

Jesus knew that what we need is an invitation, not a lecture. That's why He told the parable of the prodigal son. (See Luke 15:11–32.) It's not really just a nice story about how the Prodigal got out of his pigpen. This incredible story is designed to beckon us back to our heavenly Father's house, where a party is being thrown in our honor!

Let's review it for a moment, and I think you'll see what I mean.

From a Pigpen to a Party

You probably know the story about this wealthy man who had two sons. He greatly loved both of them, but each son had something blocking his ability to *experience* the father's love.

The younger son took his share of the inheritance and quickly squandered it in wild living. When his money ran out, he had to get a job feeding pigs, just to stay alive by eating their slops. It was in the pigpen that the young man came to his senses, assessed his options, and humbly returned home.

And this is the amazing part of the story. Instead of scolding and punishing his wayward son, the father threw him a huge *party*. Do you see how crazy this seems? The young son was a partier, and when he returned home, his father threw him the biggest party the boy had ever seen!

I'm sure the Prodigal would have returned home a lot sooner if he realized the love, acceptance, and blessings that awaited him there. He had spent all his money on partying that could never satisfy, when all along, his father had been ready to throw him a p-a-r-t-y that would change his life forever.

Let this sink in for a moment. Perhaps there's a part of your life—maybe even a *hidden* part—that is a lot like the younger son's. You were raised to know better, but you've strayed from home and left the values you know were true.

It's possible that you've hidden your tracks well, and no one even knows about the dark areas of your life that have kept you away from your heavenly Father's party. Perhaps you're addicted to porn…using illegal drugs…hooked on gambling…or covering up an affair. You're hoping no one will find out, but your secret is taking a huge toll.

My friend, you don't have to continue walking in the shadowland of compromise and sin. You can acknowledge what your heavenly Father already knows. He knows all about your pigpen, and He loves you anyway. As soon as you begin your journey home, He will run to embrace you, undeterred by the stench of where you've been.

There's no need to delay. You don't have to clean yourself up before returning to the Father's house. *Come just as you are!*

Not Just Servants, Sons

But as beautiful as it is that the young son left the pigpen and was accepted by his father, the story is not primarily about getting *out* of sin—it's about getting *into* a new life of purpose and celebration in the house of your Father. When this son witnessed the joyous music and dancing coming from his father's house, something resonated in his heart. His vision for life returned, and he remembered who he was—not just a servant, but a son.

I'm convinced that many people hang out in the pigpens of life because they've lost sight of who God has created them to be. They're like someone with amnesia who can no longer remember their name or identity.

So let me ask you...

Do you still remember the dream or calling God placed in your heart many years ago? Or has it become a distant memory, needing the fresh wind of the Holy Spirit to rekindle the fire and remind you once again of who you are?

If you know the story, you'll remember the unexpected twist at the end of Jesus' parable. While the Prodigal came home to a warm embrace and a lavish party, the older brother refused to enter into the father's house to join the celebration.

How sad! While his younger brother had once risked missing out on his destiny because of sin and worldliness, the older brother remained in bondage because of religion, self-righteousness, and unforgiveness—chains often much more difficult to break.

So be careful if you smugly look down on your brothers and sisters who have been hanging out in pigpens. Unless you humble yourself and get a better attitude, they might enter into the party while you're left outside pouting!

You see, the invitation to this party is all about grace, not perfection. You'll never be "good enough" to enter in. As the great old hymn says,

Just as I am, without one plea,
But that Thy blood was shed for me,
And that Thou bidst me come to Thee,
  O Lamb of God, I come, I come.[2]

My friend, your Father has scheduled a party in your honor. Don't let *anything* keep you from attending.

---

2. Charlotte Elliott, "Just As I Am," 1836.

SIX

HE'S STILL *TURNING WATER INTO WINE*

If I asked you where Jesus did His first miracle, what would you say? Many people would assume the first miracle happened in a synagogue or other religious gathering, or perhaps at one of Jesus' open-air sermons.

But if you think miracles only happen at religious gatherings—perhaps where there's a choir singing or a keyboard setting the atmosphere—you've got it all wrong. In fact, when Jesus performed His first miracle, there's no evidence He even read a Scripture verse.

You see, Jesus' first miracle was at a *party*. A wedding feast, to be exact. Jesus wasn't the preacher at the wedding, either. He came as one of the guests.

In the story of the Prodigal Son, we saw God as our heavenly Father, throwing a big party, complete with music, dancing, dining, and joyous celebration. In the story of the wedding feast at Cana (see John 2:1–11), we see the Son of God bringing His miracle-working power into the party others had thrown.

Too Religious

When I read stories like these, I'm always convicted that most of us are too *religious*. Jesus was widely known as the friend of sinners (see Luke 7:34), but some of us are just known as the friends of other Pharisees. We can't imagine bringing the power of God's kingdom into the marketplace where we work or to a social occasion like a wedding.

Hey, it's time to be more like Jesus!

At the wedding in Cana, Jesus miraculously turned ordinary water into extraordinary wine. This is a very encouraging principle for us today. Why? Because we *all* have "water" of some kind that needs to be transformed.

Some of us need to have our finances transformed...some of us, our health transformed...or our emotions transformed...or our families transformed. Others have lives of boredom and drudgery—and they need a transformation that brings back the zip and excitement.

And I meet lots of people who are living in bondage to some area of sin, and they need a transformation that sets them free to experience God's best for their life. Let's get real, my friend: you'll never fulfill the Lord's highest purposes for your life if you allow yourself to become addicted to drugs, alcohol, the occult, porn, or sex outside of marriage.

But believe me, I understand some things about temptation and addiction. And I *also* know the power of God can deliver any person who cries out to Him!

Sometimes temptation is born out of sheer boredom and a lack of purpose. When we don't see God's vision for our lives, we're prone to run wild into things we shouldn't be doing: "*When people do not accept divine guidance, they run wild. But whoever obeys the law is joyful*" (Proverbs 29:18 NLT). And that brings us back to the story of Jesus turning water into wine.

Ordinary to Extraordinary

Water is an essential, elemental part of life. But in this story it also stands for the plain, the ordinary, and the bland. Wine, in contrast, has flavor and fizz. Later in His ministry, Jesus said this kind of wine must be put into "*new wineskins*" (Matthew 9:17), because it needs room to expand and grow.

Take a second and ponder what boring, bland parts of your life may be due for a transformation. Your job? Your ministry? Your marriage? Your relationship with the Lord?

The good news is that Jesus can turn *ordinary* things into something *extraordinary*. If you've lost your fizz in some area of your life, He can help you get it back. And if you've been stagnating instead of expanding and growing, your turnaround can be closer than you think.

However, you need to understand that transformation comes with a price. Jesus' mother told the servants at the wedding feast, *"Whatever He says to you, do it"* (John 2:5).

Mary's statement was pretty radical statement, wasn't it? I guarantee that if you follow this profound advice, your water will surely be turned into wine. Are you willing to do *whatever* He tells you to do? Think about it. That's the price of transforming your circumstances and your life—you have to follow the Lord's instructions.

The wedding feast *"ran out of wine"* (verse 3), and perhaps that's how you're feeling today as well. You *had* money…but it ran out. You *had* love…but now it seems to be gone. You *had* dreams…but somehow they evaporated or turned into nightmares.

At such times, it's easy to feel frustrated or disillusioned. "I never thought it would be this way," you moan. That's exactly how the people at the wedding feast must have felt when they ran out of wine.

But the story isn't over yet…or at least, it doesn't have to be.

No wine? No problem! All you have to do is find out what Jesus is telling you to do. More often than not, He will tell you to give Him something you *have* (like water) in order to get something you *need* (like wine). Sounds fairly simple, doesn't it?

So what do you have today, and what do you need? Like exchanging water for wine, I promise you it will be a great exchange indeed.

Those who taste the newly made "wine" in your life may well be like the master of the feast, who *"did not know where it came from"* but loved the new wine, saying to the bridegroom, *"You have kept the good wine until now!"* (verses 9–10). They'll wonder where you got such peace, joy, and zest for life, even amid difficult times. What a great chance to tell them about Jesus, the one who can turn *their* water into wine, too.

The Best for Last

Perhaps you're tempted to feel that life has passed you by and your best years are now behind you. But this story ends with some additional good news. Jesus didn't just replace the old wine with something new: He saved the best for last! (See verse 10.) And He can do the same for you when you do what He says and give Him what you have.

Do you have hope for your future? Do you believe that God can turn things around for you and give you a great life in the days ahead? This is crucial! When you have hope for your future, it helps you to overcome temptations and break free from enemy strongholds. (See 1 John 3:8–9.)

Immediately after the story of Jesus turning water into wine at the wedding feast, we read an account of Him cleansing the temple. (See John 2:13–22.) I don't think this is any accident, because real transformation will always lead to deep cleansing and moral change.

Jesus brought the blessings of the kingdom of God to a wedding feast, reminiscent of the lavish party thrown for the Prodigal when he returned home. In contrast, He brought rebuke to the corrupt religious leaders in the outer courts of the temple, who bore a strong resemblance to the older brother who refused to enter the celebration in his father's house.

What a challenging lesson for us today. Lots of folks are plenty religious, but not really like Jesus. No wonder many people have rejected the church and chosen a life of sin! That's no excuse, of course, but perhaps it's one of the reasons you've strayed from God today.

The good news is that your heavenly Father is calling you home—not to punish you, but to forgive you and restore you. Instead of giving you *punishment*, He wants to give you a *party*!

SEVEN

THE PIT, THE PRISON, AND THE PALACE

One of the most predictable truths of life is that those who have high callings will have to overcome great trials on the road to their destiny. I wish this weren't true, but it is. If you want to have an extraordinary impact on the world, get ready for some difficult trials, often accompanied by injustices at the hands of other people.

Many biblical heroes could be cited to illustrate this principle, but the story of Joseph, the favored son of Jacob, is especially poignant.

Of all of his children, Jacob loved Joseph the most. (See Genesis 37:3.) And none of the other sons had the high calling Joseph had. So did Joseph have a soft, easy life because of this special favor from God and special bond he shared with his earthly father? Certainly not! In fact, he had to go through *extraordinary trials* in preparation for the *extraordinary impact* he was destined to one day have.

You probably know the story. When Joseph was just seventeen years old, he had some vivid dreams that provided a glimpse of his future. His brothers were already jealous of him, and the audacious dreams infuriated them to the point of violence.

First the brothers threw him in a pit. Then he was sold into slavery to some Ishmaelite traders and taken to Egypt. He ended up working for Potiphar, one of Pharaoh's officials, and things finally seemed to be on an upswing.

But it wasn't over yet. Potiphar's wife, enraged that Joseph refused to sleep with her, wrongfully accused him of attempted rape, and Joseph was condemned to thirteen years in prison. He had successfully avoided temptation, but the outcome seemed completely unfair!

One of his prison mates, a former butler to Pharoah, had a vivid dream one night that Joseph successfully interpreted to be an impending release from prison. Joseph encouraged him to put in a good word with Pharoah once he got out, but the butler forgot to mention him to the Pharoah for two whole years!

The Bible repeatedly says throughout the story, "The LORD was with Joseph" (Genesis 39:2, 21, 23)—but Joseph surely must have wondered about it at times. From our perspective, we can easily see that the numerous trials and injustices he faced were simply part of God's refining process, preparing him for future greatness. That's something for you and me to remember the next time *we* have to deal with unpleasant, unjust circumstances. God has promised to work them all together for good when we entrust our lives to Him. (See Romans 8:28.)

Joseph's story is an example of the often-stated principle: "Tough times don't last, but tough people do." This man of destiny continued to patiently trust the Lord no matter what he faced, and eventually he *outlasted* his problems.

The Key of Forgiveness

However, there's a vital key Joseph had to use in order to successfully get unstuck from the *pit* and the *prison* so he could reside in Pharaoh's *palace*—ultimately saving his family and the entire nation of Egypt from starvation.

That key is *forgiveness*.

You see, many people get stuck and bound up in life because they refuse to forgive the people who have wronged them. From a human standpoint, Joseph had every right to be angry toward his brothers who tossed him into a pit and then sold him into slavery. And it must have been difficult for him to forgive Potiphar's wife, whose lies resulted in Joseph being thrown into prison. And what about the butler? Joseph's time in prison could have been two years shorter if the butler had simply remembered to tell Pharaoh about Joseph right away.

What would have happened if Joseph had failed to forgive these people? He would have remained stuck at some point in his journey. He would have been in bondage to the past instead of being able to fulfill God's vision for his future.

Once the butler did finally tell Pharaoh about this man in prison who had the ability to interpret dreams, and Joseph was called forth to interpret the Pharaoh's troubling dreams, Joseph was placed in a position of power, authority, and responsibility. In fact, Joseph was second-in-command—his only boss was Pharaoh!

His brothers were terrified when they realized that Joseph was now the prime minister of Egypt, with power to kill them or enact any other kind of revenge. How shocked they must have been when Joseph instead assured them of his love and forgiveness—even when they clearly didn't "deserve" it.

Not only did Joseph choose not to retaliate against his brothers, but he actively treated them with unconditional love and undeserved kindness:

> *"Do not be afraid, for am I in the place of God? But as for you, you meant evil against me; but God meant it for good, in order to bring it about as it is this day, to save many people alive. Now therefore, do not be afraid; I will provide for you and your little ones." And he comforted them and spoke kindly to them.*
>
> (Genesis 50:19–21)

What a beautiful picture of God's abounding grace given to undeserving people like us, who had treated Him as our enemy! (See Romans 5:6–8.) And what an astounding revelation of God's ability to redeem even the most horrendous circumstances and turn them around for our good.

In Matthew 18:21–35, Jesus tells the story of another man who went to prison. Why? Because he refused to forgive. Not only was he *imprisoned* by his unforgiving attitude, but Jesus says he was *tortured* and *tormented*. While this may seem like an extreme outcome, it's crucial for you to see what Jesus is describing here: those who allow unforgiveness and bitterness to fester in their hearts will inevitably be bound up and tormented.

Before we move on, take a moment to allow the Holy Spirit to search your heart. Is there anyone you've not forgiven? No matter how unjustly you've been treated, your freedom and deliverance depends on extending forgiveness and setting the other person free.

I know you may have faced some horrific treatment along the way. Perhaps you've been sexually abused, physically beaten, lied about, wrongfully fired from a job, or betrayed by a spouse. But if you insist on hanging on to your hurts and offenses, you will find yourself *stuck* to the traumas of your past. Don't allow that to happen, my friend. God wants to set you free to fulfill His great plans for your future. (See Jeremiah 29:11.)

Don't wait a moment longer! Let God's forgiveness fill your heart, and then extend that forgiveness to anyone who has hurt you. You'll be glad you did.

EIGHT

RESCUED FROM SLAVERY

Everyone needs a new beginning at one time or another in their life. This may be a new beginning in your health or your finances, your emotions, or your relationships. And sometimes you might even need a new beginning in your relationship with God.

One of the most stunning stories in the Bible is the account of how the Lord gave a new beginning to an entire people group—the Israelites—after they had spent over four hundred years as slaves in Egypt. Think of how *long* this bondage had lasted, from one generation to another. Four centuries of slavery—that's even longer than the United States has been a nation!

Fortunately, God heard the cries of His people, and He had a rescue plan:

> *And I have also heard the groaning of the children of Israel whom the Egyptians keep in bondage, and I have remembered My covenant. Therefore say to the children of Israel: "I am the LORD; I will bring you out from under the burdens of the Egyptians, I will rescue you from their bondage, and I will redeem you with an outstretched arm and with great judgments."*
>
> (Exodus 6:5–6)

My friend, I'm convinced that God has heard *your* cry today, just as He heard the Israelites. But you have to be *honest* with Him about the area of your life that has been held captive. It is the truth that will set you free (see John 8:32), so you must truthfully tell the Lord about your struggles.

Honesty also means it won't do any good to blame somebody else for your troubles. You'll never find freedom if you spend all your time blaming the government, your parents, your siblings, your spouse, or your employer for the mess you find yourself in. No, you must take *responsibility* for your actions and admit your mistakes.

Perhaps it hard for you to acknowledge that the devil has a stronghold in your life. "Oh, I like to have a few drinks, but it's not really a problem," you say. Or when someone implies that you've been physically abusing your spouse or girlfriend, you reply, "I don't have any anger issues. She just likes to push my buttons."

Over my decades of ministry, I run into countless people who are still in some form of bondage or addiction. Although slavery was abolished in America over a century ago, countless people are still captive as slaves to the devil in some area of their life.

But notice the three things God promised the Israelites: *"I will bring you out…I will rescue you…I will redeem you."* Do you see how powerful these promises are and how relevant they are to your life today? Rather than just telling you to try harder or pick yourself up by your bootstraps, the Lord says, "I WILL…."

It doesn't matter what you're going through or how long you've been a captive. When the Lord has spoken, He will watch over His word and bring it to pass. (See Jeremiah 1:12 NASB.) Every victory and turnaround in life begins with a promise from the Lord, and that's why He has given us His written Word and His Spirit.

Know this: God has heard your groaning. He is not oblivious to your situation. He feels your pain, sees your tears, and cares about your challenges. The Bible says God remembered His covenant toward the Israelites—and He remembers His promises to you, as well.

When God assured Moses that He heard the cries of the Israelites, the Hebrew word for *heard* means "to be granted." In other words, God not only has heard your petitions, but He wants to grant you the breakthrough you need as you hold on to His promises.

God assured His people, *"I will rescue you."* Let that sink in for a moment. It means that no matter what kind of mess you find yourself in today, this can be your season to be rescued by the Almighty God! The Lord will rescue you and bring you out of your captivity, just as He did for the Israelites.

Psalm 30:5 says, *"His anger lasts only a moment, but his favor lasts a lifetime! Weeping may last through the night, but joy comes with the morning"* (NLT). No matter how long your trials have lasted or how many tears you've shed, this can be the day His favor dawns in your life!

As God fulfilled His promises to the Israelites, He will do the same for *you*. Every promise will come to pass as you choose to put your trust in the Lord.

Hold on to the promises in His Word today. Follow His instructions and put your trust in Him. When you do, you will see supernatural breakthroughs manifest in your life.

Never give up on God, for He will never give up on you. No matter how dark the night has been, a new day is at hand. I declare a new season in your life, in Jesus' mighty name!

NINE

APPLYING THE PROMISES

God has given us wonderful promises for our deliverance, but they usually have to be activated by obeying His instructions and learning His processes. That's why many believers end up disappointed and disillusioned. They're waiting for God to fulfill His promises, while *He's* waiting for *them* to obey some instruction He's given them.

As we've already seen, God promised the Israelites: *"I will bring you out...I will rescue you...I will redeem you"* (Exodus 6:6). But the story didn't end there. The Lord gave His people detailed instructions for how they would gain freedom from their slavery.

The first step in the Israelites' liberation was to observe the first Feast of Passover. Right from the onset, God made it clear that this was to be a time of new beginnings: *"This month shall be your beginning of months; it shall be the first month of the year to you"* (Exodus 12:2). Notice that when God spoke these words, the Israelites were still living as slaves in the land of Egypt. They clearly *needed* a new beginning—and perhaps you do as well. But the odds certainly seemed to be against them.

The Power of the Blood

During the first Passover feast, the blood of the lamb was sprinkled on the doorposts of the Israelites' homes, and this blood protected them from the death angel that struck the Egyptians. God gave His people a powerful promise, which can still transform our lives today through the blood of Jesus:

Then the whole assembly of the congregation of Israel shall kill [the Passover lamb] at twilight. And they shall take some of the blood and put it on the two doorposts and on the lintel of the houses where they eat it.... For I will pass through the land of Egypt on that night, and will strike all the firstborn in the land of Egypt, both man and beast; and against all the gods of Egypt I will execute judgment: I am the LORD. *Now the blood shall be a sign for you on the houses where you are. And when I see the blood, I will pass over you; and the plague shall not be on you to destroy you when I strike the land of Egypt.*

(Exodus 12:6–7, 12–13)

Do you see the supernatural protection you have when you choose to apply the blood of Jesus to the doorposts of your heart, your mind, your body, your family, your finances, and every other aspect of your life?

When the thief comes to steal, kill, and destroy...

When the devil comes as a roaring lion, seeking someone to devour...

When demons of sickness, poverty, lust, addiction, fear, or depression look for someone to prey upon...

They will have to go past you and find someone else to attack!

Although preaching on "the power of the blood" isn't very fashionable these days, the Bible says *"without shedding of blood there is no remission* [forgiveness]" (Hebrews 9:22). This theme has been described as a "scarlet thread" that extends throughout the entire Bible, from Genesis to Revelation.

Do you see how the scarlet thread and the blood of the Passover lamb beautifully foreshadow what Jesus did for us on the cross? Through His incredible mercy and grace, He shed His blood to purchase our salvation, protection, and favor. Yet the cross was also a picture of God's fierce judgment of sin. As Passover struck a devastating blow to the false gods of the Egyptians, the cross forever crippled Satan's evil kingdom: *"Having disarmed principalities and powers, He made a public spectacle of them, triumphing over them in it"* (Colossians 2:15).

A Fresh Start

So, do you need a fresh start in some area of your life? Have you been held captive by Satan's schemes, hindering you from your calling as a son or daughter of God? Then I encourage you to remember the example of Passover and its later fulfillment at the cross: Declare that you are placing the blood of Jesus, God's perfect Passover Lamb, on the doorposts of your heart.

Then take the next step, claiming the power of Jesus' blood to *break every chain* that has bound your health, finances, relationships, or emotions. Recognize that His blood is more powerful than your addictions, your fears, and your insecurities.

This surefire strategy for victory over Satan's snares is echoed in Revelation 12:11: *"They overcame* [the devil] *by the blood of the Lamb and by the word of their testimony, and they did not love their lives to the death."*

Of course, the blood referred to here as *"the blood of the Lamb"* is the blood of Jesus, *"the Lamb of God who takes away the sin of the world"* (John 1:29). So remember: originally foreshadowed in the Feast of Passover, Jesus' blood is a crucial weapon in your arsenal against Satan. It's the seal of your salvation, the proof of your forgiveness, and the sign of your covenant relationship with almighty God.

The devil is aptly described as *"the accuser"* (Revelation 12:10), but his accusations are nullified whenever you apply the blood of Jesus to your life. No matter how many mistakes you've made in the past, you can be certain that *"There is therefore now no condemnation to those who are in Christ Jesus"* (Romans 8:1).

Take a few minutes right now to pause and pray, making sure *"the blood of the Lamb"* has been applied to every area of your life. Be certain you aren't basing your relationship with God on your own goodness but on the scarlet cord that testifies of Jesus' death on your behalf.

Then go ahead and claim the powerful truth of Revelation 12:11 over your life by declaring: "I am overcoming Satan by the blood of the Lamb and by the word of my testimony, because I will not love my own life, even when faced with death!"

The Lord hasn't planned any defeats for you, my friend. He has given you *"the blood of the Lamb"* and other powerful spiritual weapons to defeat the enemy. When you accept the full benefits of what Jesus did for you on the cross, you can follow Him into a life of triumph and blessing: *"Thanks be to God, who always leads us in triumph in Christ, and manifests through us the sweet aroma of the knowledge of Him in every place"* (2 Corinthians 2:14 NASB).

This victorious life is God's will for *you*! Draw near to Him today. Learn to use the powerful weapons He has given you to defeat the enemy and enter into a life of abundance. He wants to set you free today from anything that is hindering you from enjoying His favor and His overflowing blessings.

TEN

TAKE BACK WHAT THE ENEMY STOLE

When I share with people how they can find freedom in Christ and live in victory, I'm often asked a very important question: "Bishop Bloomer, although it's great to know I can defeat the devil in my life today, what about all the things I've already lost to him along the way? Is it too late to take back what the enemy has stolen from me?"

That's a great question, isn't it? Perhaps you've been asking yourself the same thing! Maybe you've been attacked in your family, your health, your finances, or your peace of mind—and you surely could use a miracle from God to recover your losses.

Well, I have good news! Even though the thief may have robbed you (see John 10:10), God wants to restore whatever has been stolen. The Bible is full of stories about people who were empowered to take back what the enemy had stolen. The account of what happened right after the Passover is a great example.

Remember, the first Passover was instituted by God when the Israelites had been in slavery in Egypt for over four hundred years. For many generations, the Lord's people had suffered cruel oppression—but that was about to change in a quite dramatic fashion. When the Egyptians' firstborns died at the hand of the angel of the Lord, Pharaoh finally let the people go. Even better, the Egyptians *paid* them to leave!

The people of Israel did as Moses had instructed; they asked the Egyptians for clothing and articles of silver and gold. The Lord caused the Egyptians to look favorably on the Israelites, and they

> *gave the Israelites whatever they asked for. So they stripped the Egyptians of their wealth!*   (Exodus 12:35–36 NLT)

What an amazing turnaround. For hundreds of years, the Egyptians had been their cruel captors, and now the Israelites were asking not just for *freedom*, but for *reparations* as well. Remarkably, *God's favor* brought about favor even from the *enemies* of His people.

The Israelites had been robbed of their blessings for centuries, but now they left their captivity with unimaginable riches and prosperity. Instead of being paupers and beggars, they were abundantly blessed with silver, gold, clothing, and livestock. (See verses 35–38.)

Friend, this is a powerful illustration of God's desire to turn around *your* negative circumstances and bless you beyond your wildest dreams. Even if you have been in some kind of spiritual, financial, or relational captivity for a long time, your breakthrough can come with stunning speed. When you are willing to follow God's instructions, you can confidently expect to take back what the enemy has stolen from you.

Biblical Examples

As you set your heart to obey the Lord and believe His promises, I encourage you to meditate on these great biblical examples of people who "plundered" the enemy and recovered *everything* that had been stolen:

+ Abraham recovered *everything* the enemy stole from Lot. (See Genesis 14:16.)

+ David recovered *everything* the enemy stole from Ziklag. (See 1 Samuel 30:18–19.)

+ God's law says a thief must pay back even *more* than what he stole. (See Exodus 22:1, 7.)

+ Job was blessed with *double* of everything Satan had stolen from him. (See Job 42:10.)

There's an amazing pattern here I don't want you to miss: God not only has redeemed you and me by Jesus' death on the cross, He has *also* redeemed our "stuff"—the things stolen by Satan along the way.

So if the devil has stolen something from you, don't assume it's gone forever. Take a moment and recommit your life fully to the Lord. Ask Him to give you His perspective and His strategies for overcoming the enemy's attacks. Take Him at His Word that He will reverse your losses and bless you with His presence, power, and provision.

In the book of Joel, God promised to restore even *years* of the enemy's plunder. (See Joel 2:24–26.) In Joel's time, the people of Judah faced several years of devastating attacks on their crops by locusts. Because these attacks were both severe and long-lasting, it was easy for people to lose hope:

> *What the chewing locust left, the swarming locust has eaten; what the swarming locust left, the crawling locust has eaten; and what the crawling locust left, the consuming locust has eaten.... He has **laid waste** My vine, and **ruined** My fig tree; he has **stripped it bare** and **thrown it away;** its branches are made white.*   (Joel 1:4, 7)

Perhaps the attacks of the enemy have left you feeling like this today: "laid waste...ruined...stripped bare...and thrown away." But God knows about your situation and wants to restore everything you've lost:

> *I **will restore** to you the **years** that the swarming locust has eaten, the crawling locust, the consuming locust, and the chewing locust.*   (Joel 2:25)

And when the Lord says He wants to restore what you've lost, this means a life of incredible blessing and abundance:

> *The threshing floors shall be **full** of wheat, and the vats shall **overflow** with new wine and oil.... You shall **eat in plenty** and be **satisfied,** and praise the name of the LORD your God, who has **dealt wondrously with you;** and **My people shall never be put to shame.***   (Joel 2:24, 26)

This is great news, isn't it? No matter what your past has been like, God can restore your fortunes, take away your shame, and give you a bright future.

Has the devil stolen something from your life? Your health? Your marriage? Your children? Your job? Your finances? Your vision? Your peace of mind or intimacy with the Lord? If so, there's no need to get stuck in a "victim" mentality. God wants to bless you, restore what you've lost, and give you even *more* than you had before.

Take a moment right now and recommit your life fully to the Lord. Ask Him to give you His perspective and His strategies for overcoming the enemy's attacks. Take Him at His Word that He will reverse your losses and bless you with His presence, power, and provision!

ELEVEN

HAVE YOU ACCEPTED YOUR FREEDOM?

Before we go any further, I need to challenge you about something: Do you really *believe* God's promises about the freedom He's given you through the blood of Jesus? I'm asking because I've met lots of Christians who've been in church for years, yet they somehow have missed out on applying the Bible's promises to the practical areas of their life.

I once heard the story of a young slave boy who lived on a cotton plantation in the Deep South. His parents had died, and an old man—who also worked on the plantation as a slave—had assumed the responsibility of raising the boy.

One of the boy's daily chores was to get the newspaper from the front entrance of the plantation and bring it to his master's house. In the process, he would stop by the old man's slave quarters, where this elderly mentor taught him the alphabet, how to put words and sentences together, and eventually how to read.

It was the time of the Civil War in the United States. Both of them were aware of the fierce battles being fought, and they often heard the firing of rifles and cannons in the distance. But the plantation offered a sense of isolation from the bloody battlefields nearby.

Then one chilly morning in January 1863, the boy opened the front page of the newspaper and saw two large words he couldn't pronounce and didn't understand. They were set in type about six inches high, so he knew these words must be important.

He ran to the old man and asked, "What do these words mean?"

The two words blazoned across the top of the paper read: "Emancipation Proclamation."

The old slave hesitated and then said firmly, "You don't need to know."

"Why?" the boy replied. "Those are *big* letters. Something very important must have happened."

Finally, the old man explained, "It says President Lincoln has signed an order to set all the slaves free." Then he added, "But this is a trick. You can't trust what the paper says. They just want us to become runaways so they can catch us and punish us more harshly."

The young boy adamantly disagreed. "That can't be true," he said. "If it says in the newspaper that I'm free, then *I'm free!* I'm leaving this place today, and I'm never coming back!"

The old man tried to counsel him to stay, but the boy insisted, "I'm not staying here another day."

The boy didn't deliver the paper to his master that day. Instead, he placed it along with his meager belongings in a satchel and ran from the plantation as fast as he could, never to return.

The sad part of the story is that the old man simply couldn't believe the headlines. He distrusted what the paper said, and couldn't fathom that the blood of tens of thousands of young Americans, shed on his behalf, had truly purchased his freedom. Nor could he comprehend that a single order from the president could change his destiny forever.

So the old slave stayed behind and served his master for the rest of his life. Legally, he was a free man, yet he chose not to believe the proclamation he had read in the paper. Tragically, he lived and died a slave.

However, the young boy made a life-changing decision. He believed the words in the newspaper were *true*—that President Lincoln had indeed signed a proclamation that set him free. But not only did the boy *believe* in the president's proclamation, he also *acted on his belief.* You see, faith is not just a fact—it's an *act!*

Choose Freedom

Today, you face a choice similar to the old man and the boy. You can choose to remain a slave to sin, sickness, poverty, addiction, fear, depression, worry—or whatever else is holding you in its grip—or you can choose to believe the proclamation of God's Word that you've been set free.

Are you ready to believe the Good News of God's Word? Here's the truth:

Christ died on the cross not only to pay the penalty for your sins, but also to set you *FREE*!

It took only three words for Jesus to announce *His* "Emancipation Proclamation" on the cross of Calvary. He looked up to His Father and said, *"It is finished!"* (John 19:30). At that incredible moment, the cost of your freedom was marked "Paid in full!"

Because you were purchased out of bondage by the precious blood of Christ, Satan no longer has any claim over you. No longer does he have any right to interfere with your life or enslave you to *anything* that is keeping you from God's best for your life.

In Jesus Christ you've been declared *"free indeed"* (John 8:36). So if you're still keeping one foot in the devil's plantation, it's time to leave!

Your liberty begins when you make a decision to believe the truth of what God says about you in His Word: *"You will know the truth, and the truth will set you free"* (John 8:32 NLT).

You see, the boy in the story chose to *believe* the report of his emancipation, and he took *action* accordingly. If you truly grasp the incredible price Jesus paid for your freedom, it will be impossible to remain in bondage to Satan's snares.

Friend, today can be the beginning of your freedom from sin or addiction...from depression or despair...from toxic or broken relationships...from poverty or disease. And when you believe the truth about your liberation, you can get unstuck from whatever has held you back from fulfilling God's highest purpose for your life.

TWELVE

BE LOOSED FROM A FALSE IDENTITY

I meet so many people who are confused or frustrated about their identity. Often they've been given negative labels by other people— labeled as a loser or a problem child, labeled as someone who is destined to fail rather than destined to succeed, labeled as an annoyance rather than a blessing.

What makes these negative labels so destructive is that they often come from people who are in a position of considerable influence in our lives—people such as our parents, our grandparents, our siblings, or our teachers at school.

Even if you've come from a good family, I'm sure you've gone through some hurtful experiences of one kind or another. And how you *handle* those experiences will have a lot to do in determining your character and your destiny.

The heroes in the Bible didn't have easy or trouble-free lives. Far from it. Each of them had things they needed to *overcome* in order to find their true identity and succeed in God's calling for their life.

One of these intriguing heroes is a man called Jabez. We read in 1 Chronicles 4:9–10:

> *Jabez was more honorable than his brothers; and his mother called his name Jabez, saying, "Because I bore him in pain." And Jabez called on the God of Israel, saying, "Oh that You would bless me indeed, and enlarge my territory, and that Your hand would be with me, and that You would keep me from evil, that I may not cause pain!" So God granted him what he requested.*

More Honorable

The context of this description is quite stunning—something few commentators seem to notice. This brief summary of Jabez's life is found in the midst of a genealogy of countless other people. In most cases we are only given their names, because nothing notable seems to have been accomplished by their lives.

This should be a challenge to each of us! There are currently more than 7 *billion* people on planet earth. They all have names. All are important to God. And the Lord has designed an important destiny for each of them. However, not everyone is aware of God's love or His calling. Even many believers are missing out on God's best for their lives. Instead of standing out from the crowd—like Jabez did—they are content to just blend in.

What about you? Are you content to just be a name on the genealogy list, or are you determined to stand out from the crowd and take bold steps of faith to change the world for Christ? We're told that Jabez was different from crowd and even *"more honorable"* than his own brothers.

This is really hard for many people today. There is a lot of peer pressure just to blend in and become average instead of exceptional.... ordinary instead of extraordinary.

Perhaps you've heard about the crab bucket phenomenon. If you put a bunch of crabs in a bucket, they will never escape it. Why? Because when one crab starts to climb out of the bucket, the other crabs pull him back down! If there was just one crab in the bucket, he could easily escape—but not when he's surrounded by others who want to keep him down on their level.

God is calling you to do great things, to be exceptional, to be a world-changer! Don't allow yourself to be just another crab in the bucket. You need to surround yourself with people who motivate you to dream bigger, climb higher, and to press on to God's high calling in your life.

Most of the other people in the 1 Chronicles 4 genealogy seem to have made little impact on the world. In addition to their names, their tombstones probably included just the year of their birth and the year of their death—nothing more!

You see, on this earth, we each have a date of birth and a date of death. In between is just a dash—and that dash represents what we *done* during our journey on the planet. Have we impacted lives through our words and deeds? Have we made the world a better place? Have we brought souls into God's kingdom through sharing the gospel?

I love the old statement by missionary C. T. Studd: "Only one life, 'twill soon be past. Only what's done for Christ will last." C. T. Studd knew that the dash on our tombstone is supposed to count for something—something great—something that lasts for eternity.

It's amazing that several thousand years after Jabez's life, we're still talking about his legacy. If Jesus tarries another ten, twenty, or even one hundred years, I hope each of us will have an enduring legacy like this. But that will never happen unless we're intent on breaking free from the commonplace, trivial pursuits of humanity in order to stand out and truly make a difference.

Pain and Rejection

As we continue reading about Jabez's life, we realize this was no easy thing for him. His life got off to a rough start, and it seemed like the cards were stacked against him. His birth was so painful that *"his mother called his name Jabez"*—derived from the Hebrew word for *pain*.

You might be able to relate to Jabez's story at this point. Your parents probably didn't name you "a pain"—at least not formally! But let's be honest: Sometimes parents, siblings, peers, pastors, or employers send us negative messages about our identity, about who we are. Or maybe it was a bully in your neighborhood who called you too skinny, too fat, too ugly, too short, or too stupid.

There's an old saying that is totally false. I'm sure you've heard it: "Sticks and stones can break my bones, but words can never hurt me." The truth is just the opposite: we can recover from sticks and stones and even broken bones—but people's words often cause us a lifetime of hurt.

That's how Jabez's story begins: with pain and rejection from the very people who should have shown him the most love and acceptance. But the good news is that Jabez wasn't content to wallow in his situation. He rejected the labels put on him by his detractors, choosing instead to seek God for a new identity, a new purpose, and a new destiny.

How did *your* story begin in its early chapters? Perhaps you had a wonderful, loving family that cared for you and nurtured you all along the way. But I meet so many people today who have had an experience more like Jabez. They are desperate to find a way to turn their pain into purpose.

Called Upon the Lord

So what did Jabez do to break free from the negative labels that threatened to bind him to a life of failure or mediocrity? First Chronicles 4:10 says, *"Jabez called on the God of Israel."*

This is such a powerful statement. If you are going to break free from people's opinions about you, you must cry out for a *higher* opinion—the opinion of Almighty God. In the end, it's really just His opinion that matters, isn't it? When you stand before Him in eternity, the bullies and naysayers won't be there to tear you down. The only thing that will matter will be hear His beautiful words of affirmation, *"Well done, good and faithful servant!"* (Matthew 25:21).

My friend, perhaps you need a name change today, a new identity. God can take your pain and make you a prince or a princess. He can take your failures and give you a glorious future.

But you have a role to play. You must cry out to Him, like Jabez did. You may even need to wrestle with Him, not letting go until you have a new name, a fresh start, a new beginning.

Throughout the Bible, we see the Lord changing people's names in order to restore them to their true identity. Abram became Abraham. Sarai became Sarah. Jacob became Israel. Simon became Peter. Levi became Matthew. Saul became Paul. Joseph became Barnabas.

You see, you don't have to be *stuck* with the names or labels people have put on you! In Christ, you can become a new creation— liberated to wear a new name and new identity.

Enlarge the Territory

Notice that Jabez asked God to *"enlarge his territory"* (1 Chronicles 4:10). In the same way, God wants to enlarge *you* today. He wants to give you bigger dreams, higher visions, and more audacious plans. It's time to grow up!

But think of how incredible this prayer request must have been for Jabez, the man who was labeled a pain and a loser. He could have curled up in a ball and wallowed in his victimhood, but instead he did just the opposite. He called on God to *enlarge* his territory and give him greater responsibilities and impact.

So what about you? Is there some area of your life that you need God to enlarge? Your career...your finances...your health...your relationships...your ministry...your vision? Today can be your first step in asking God for an *increase* that will change your entire trajectory in life.

Keep from Harm

Jabez's final request was that God would keep from *harm*—from the things that would cause pain, either to himself or the people around him. Jabez was a man of great faith, but he also was a realist. He understood that he had received a legacy of pain and dysfunction, and the natural thing would be to continue that legacy in his own life.

It's no secret that people in pain tend to cause pain to others. People who have been abused often become abusers. Children of alcoholics and addicts too often follow in their parents' footsteps.

But Jabez knew the negative patterns must stop! He had been called a pain, but that's not how he wanted to treat others.

You need to know that whatever painful legacies you've received can stop—and they can stop now. It's time to cry out to God and make a decision that life will be different from this day forward.

First Peter 1:18 says, *"You were ransomed from the futile ways inherited from your forefathers"* (ESV). Isn't that fantastic news? You don't have to follow in the pathways of pain and failure you may have inherited. Nor do you have to remain stuck because of your own mistakes and bad decisions in the past.

Although Jabez got off to a rough start in life, that's not how his story ended. This passage about Jabez ends with a beautiful conclusion: *"God granted him what he requested"* (1 Chronicles 4:10).

I love happy endings, don't you? Just as God did in the life of Jabez, He has planned a happy ending for *you*! It's a new day, time for a fresh start. God is offering to set you free from all the old, negative labels of your past.

Get ready to step into your new identity and purpose!

THIRTEEN

STAND IN YOUR TRUE IDENTITY

God graciously set Jabez free from the label he had been given by his mother—the label of being someone who causes other people pain. This was an amazing turnaround, especially since Jabez didn't have the full Scriptures to help him see God's perspective on his life.

You and I shouldn't struggle with this nearly as much as we often do, or as Jabez did, because from cover to cover, the Bible reveals our true identity as beloved sons and daughters of the living God. So we might as well tear up any false ID we've been carrying around.

A Simple Prayer

Now, this book was written with the assumption that you've already given your life to Jesus Christ and have an assurance of your forgiveness and salvation. But before we continue, it's important to take a few minutes to make sure this is really true of your life.

The Bible says, *"If you confess with your mouth the Lord Jesus and believe in your heart that God raised Him from the dead, you will be saved"* (Romans 10:9). So when you confess and believe these truths, the Bible promises that you'll receive God's gift of eternal life. You'll have a home in heaven with Him after you die, and you'll *also* receive the blessings of His peace, presence, power, protection, and provision while you're here on earth.

If you've never asked Jesus to be the Lord of your life, you can pray this simple prayer right now:

Dear Jesus,

I need You. I confess that I'm a sinner and that You are holy. Jesus, I believe you are God's Son and that He raised You from the dead.

Thank You for dying on the cross for me and for providing the only way for me to have a relationship with You as my heavenly Father. Please forgive me for all my sins, and wash me clean with Your blood. Come and live in my heart now, and fill me with Your Holy Spirit.

Thank You for rescuing me and giving me the opportunity to live in heaven with You forever. Please be the Lord of my life. Teach me how to love You and walk with You every day.

I pray this in Your name. Amen.

If you've truly prayed this prayer, you have been "born again" and saved by God's amazing grace. The angels in heaven are rejoicing right now over *you.* I welcome you to the family of God!

When you have a relationship with the Lord, it's important for you to spend time with Him every day. Read His Word and talk with Him. Sit quietly and listen for the voice of His Holy Spirit to speak to you. And learn to be aware of His presence with you, moment by moment.

The Truth About Your Identity

As you grow and mature in your faith and your knowledge of the Bible, you will learn to recognize God's voice speaking to you in your mind and heart. He will bring you wonderful comfort and direction for your life as you gain a greater understanding of His Word. And day by day, He will unfold more of His wonderful plans for you. (See Jeremiah 29:11–12.)

Because you have prayed to surrender your life to Christ as your Lord and Savior, God's Word declares many incredible truths about your new identity. No matter what you may have done before being born again in Christ, in Him you are now a *"new creation,"* and Scripture says, *"Old things have passed away; behold, all things have become new"* (2 Corinthians 5:17).

In order to have an effective prayer life, it's crucial that you understand who you are in Christ. Only then will you have boldness to claim God's promises and stand in His authority.

I encourage you to take time to look up and meditate on these amazing verses about your new identity in Christ. By faith, agree with what God's Word says about you, and claim His promises to you as His dear child.

In Christ, you are...

+ Justified, forgiven, and redeemed (Romans 3:24; Ephesians 1:7).

+ Crucified to your old, sinful self and raised to a new life (Romans 6:6; Ephesians 2:5; Colossians 3:1).

+ Free from condemnation (Romans 8:1).

+ Free from the law of sin and death (Romans 8:2).

+ Accepted by God (Ephesians 1:6).

+ Sanctified, holy, and set apart for God's purposes (1 Corinthians 6:11).

+ Filled with wisdom, righteousness, sanctification, and redemption (1 Corinthians 1:30).

+ Led in constant triumph (2 Corinthians 2:14).

+ Liberated (Galatians 5:1).

+ Joined with other believers in God's family (Ephesians 2:11–22).

+ An heir of God (Galatians 4:7; Ephesians 1:11).

+ Blessed with every spiritual blessing (Ephesians 1:3).

+ Chosen, holy, and blameless before God (Ephesians 1:4).

+ Sealed with the Holy Spirit (Ephesians 1:13).

+ Seated in a heavenly position (Ephesians 2:6).

+ God's workmanship, created for a life that bears good fruit (Ephesians 2:10; John 15:5).

+ Near to God (Ephesians 2:13).

+ A partaker of God's promises (Ephesians 3:6).

+ Bold and confident in approaching God (Ephesians 3:12).

+ Transferred from spiritual darkness into God's light (Ephesians 5:8).

+ A member of the body of Christ (Ephesians 5:30).

+ Hidden with Christ in God (Colossians 3:3).

+ Guarded in your heart and mind by God's peace (Philippians 4:7).

+ Perfectly provided for, with all your needs supplied (Philippians 4:19).

+ Complete (Colossians 2:10).

As you meditate on what God says about you in His Word, you will be *"transformed by the renewing of your mind"* (Romans 12:2). Satan's lies and accusations about you will be replaced by your new identity as *"the righteousness of God"* in Christ (2 Corinthians 5:21).

Remember this great promise from God to those who meditate on His Word and receive it as truth in their lives:

Blessed is the man who walks not in the counsel of the ungodly, nor stands in the path of sinners, nor sits in the seat of the scornful; but his delight is in the law of the LORD, and in His law he meditates day and night. He shall be like a tree planted by the rivers of water, that brings forth its fruit in its season, whose leaf also shall not wither; and whatever he does shall prosper.

(Psalm 1:1–3)

Be bold in claiming biblical promises like this. As you delight in God's Word and walk in His ways, you will prosper and be blessed!

Your thoughts must increasingly be shaped by God's truth, because your thoughts determine the person you will become. That's why Solomon pointed out, *"As he thinks in his heart, so is he"* (Proverbs 23:7).

Never forget that the devil is a liar. (See John 8:44.) He will lie about God, and he will lie about *you*. It's crucial that you know and stand upon the *truth* about your new identity in Christ!

FOURTEEN

ESCAPE FROM
THE HOUSE OF MIRRORS

If you've ever visited a carnival or amusement park, you may gone to a House of Mirrors. It's a place where everything is distorted. Fat people looked skinny, skinny people looked fat, and *everyone* looks strange. Although you can recognize yourself in the twisted mirrors, you know it's not an accurate picture of what you really look like.

If we don't stand in our true identity in Christ—what God says about us in His Word—we're in jeopardy of living our life in a House of Mirrors. The Bible is supposed to be the mirror where we find our self-image (see James 1:22–25, 1 Corinthians 13:12), but too often we see ourselves through the twisted lenses of the people around us.

If you take a moment to think about it, I'm sure you know many people who see themselves in a very distorted ways:

+ They're not stupid…but they *see themselves* as stupid.

+ They're not victims…but they *see themselves* as victims.

+ They're not too fat…but they *see themselves* as too fat.

+ They're not too skinny…but they *see themselves* as too skinny.

+ They're not failures…but they *see themselves* as failures.

+ They're not unloved…but they *see themselves* as unloved.

Even though it might be fun visiting the House of Mirrors on occasion, it sure isn't fun to live your life there. No matter what kind of warped self-image we may have received from our parents, siblings, schoolteachers, or friends, the Lord wants to heal how we see ourselves. He wants us to have healthy self-esteem so we don't continually sabotage our success.

A Healthy Self-Esteem

Self-esteem is our personal opinion of our own worth, competence, and importance. It includes our thoughts, feelings, and attitudes toward ourselves. Sometimes our self-image is based on true facts about our personality or looks, but often our self-image has nothing at all to do with reality. The "mirrors" we are using to evaluate our worth are twisted and distorted.

Do you see how important self-esteem is? It affects every area of your life! A poor self-image will pollute your thoughts, emotions, actions, and values. It will make you feel hopeless, unwanted, unneeded, and unloved. You will constantly feel sorry for yourself and will end up pulling away from other people.

Your level of self-esteem will cause you to react either positively or negatively toward other people. Those who have a healthy self-image will be outgoing and encouraging toward others, while those with poor self-esteem will tend to be jealous, insecure, and possessive.

Your self-image also plays a major role in your ability to fulfill your dreams. A negative self-image will destroy your creativity and motivation, making you feel useless and depressed. You will find yourself unable to embark on new ventures, because your negative attitude toward yourself will make every new idea seem destined to fail.

If the truth were known, almost everyone has struggled with a poor self-image at one time or another. We feel unsuccessful and worthless, when God sees us as full of great potential and value. Many of us—especially if we're male—still try to keep up our macho image, but inside we're more insecure and vulnerable than anyone can imagine.

When we are feeling low about our self-image, it is easy to think we are the only ones who feel that way. Those around us may seem like they have it all together, while we are the "ugly duckling," the loser no one wants to hang out with. Believe it or not, *everyone* has felt this way at one time or another. You are certainly not alone in the struggle for a better self-image.

So how do you know if you have healthy self-esteem? There are clear indicators. A person with a good self-image...

+ Doesn't give up easily, even after failure, but is able to keep going and learn from the effort.

+ Is willing to take risks, confident that success will come in the end.

+ Knows what they want and isn't embarrassed to ask for it.

+ Chooses good relationships with people who are emotionally and spiritually healthy.

+ Can hang out with others without losing their own sense of self.

+ Has discovered the joy of helping others instead of being wrapped up with themselves.

Change Is Possible

So how are you doing with your self-image? If you're struggling, here's good news: *Your self-image isn't something you're stuck with forever!* You weren't born with a negative self-image, and if you have one now, you don't need to keep it. Countless people who are successful and happy today were once timid and self-destructive.

One remarkable example of this is TV and movie star Oprah Winfrey. Much of her life, she struggled with being overweight. Yet it is hard to find a person today who has a more positive image of herself. This is even more amazing when you look at her difficult childhood.

Oprah was born in Kosciusko, Mississippi, to unmarried teenage parents. After first living in poverty on her grandmother's farm, at age six she began staying on and off with her mother in Milwaukee. There she was sexually abused by male relatives. At age fourteen, Oprah gave birth to a premature baby who didn't survive. She then went to live with her father and stepmother in Nashville, where she finally began to thrive.

At her new home in Nashville, Oprah focused on her school work and did so well that she was even able to skip several grades. She earned a scholarship to Tennessee State University and, while still in school, landed a job as co-anchor of the evening news at WTF-TV. Eventually she became the hostess of the nation's most popular TV talk show, and then the world's highest-paid entertainer.

Based on her difficult childhood, would you have predicted success for Oprah Winfrey? It may surprise you to learn that Oprah never doubted that she would reach the top. "All my life I have known I was born to greatness," she has said.

And how has Oprah managed to accept her body, imperfect as it may be? Perhaps because her focus is more on *helping others* than on perfecting herself. As a result, she has become one of the world's most influential people.

What an encouraging story! Oprah wasn't about to let her self-worth be determined by the negative House of Mirrors where she grew up. If you've been making excuses about how your childhood traumas prohibit you from a successful future, you need to think again.

However, before you can be set free from the crazy views you've formed of yourself in the House of Mirrors, you must face the *truth* about who you really are. It may not be a fun experience to face your true self, but the truth will set you free and enable you to grow into the person you really want to be.

Renowned twentieth-century Christian author A. W. Tozer lists seven things we can ask ourselves in order to discover what we are really like:

1. What do we want the most?
2. What do we think about the most?
3. How do we use our money?
4. What do we do with our spare time?
5. Who are the people we hang out with?

6.   Who and what do we admire?

7.   What do we laugh at?

When you look at these seven areas of your life, what kind of person do you see? Do you like the person reflected in your mirror? Do you see yourself as you really are, or is your self-image clouded by negative views that aren't based in reality? Do you have any trustworthy friends or counselors who can give you some honest and objective advice on this?

I'll admit, it's hard to find a reliable mirror in a world that often tells us lies about ourselves. Yet I've found that the Bible is a mirror that always tells me the truth about who I am. (See James 1:23–25.) Friends change. Feelings change. Even our bodies change. But the Bible is a solid rock that always remains the same.

Is there hope for a transformation of your self-image? Absolutely! Look what happens when the Spirit of the Lord sets you free to be your true self:

> *The Lord is the Spirit; and where the **Spirit of the Lord** is, there is **liberty**. But we all, with unveiled face, **beholding as in a mirror the glory of the Lord**, are being **transformed** into the **same image** from glory to glory, just as by the Spirit of the Lord.*   (2 Corinthians 3:17–18)

My friend, when you focus your attention on Jesus instead of on your flaws and failures, you will increasingly become like Him. But you may need to throw away the faulty mirrors that have hindered you from becoming the person God created you to be.

FIFTEEN

IT'S TIME TO FLY

When you gave your life to Jesus Christ as your Lord and Savior, you became God's beloved son or daughter. The Bible says you were *"born of God"* (John 1:13 NIV), and you now have His spiritual DNA.

Of course, you still have choices to make as to whether you will allow God's character and DNA to be manifested in your life, but the verdict is already in regarding your ultimate destiny: *"Whom He foreknew, He also predestined to be conformed to the image of His Son"* (Romans 8:29).

Yes, you may experience setbacks and failures along the way. Sometimes your progress may be "two steps forward, one step back." But God will be relentless until you've been restored to His likeness. (See Genesis 1:26–28.)

The Bible says God *"began a good work in you."* Yet the good news doesn't stop there. The verse goes on to promise that He *"will carry it on to completion until the day of Christ Jesus"* (Philippians 1:6 NIV). Aren't you glad to know that God *finishes* what He *starts!*

My friend, God's DNA is not designed for failure and frustration, but rather for greatness, love, holiness, and victory. However, out of ignorance of what the Bible says about their DNA as God's children, many Christians base their view of themselves on their past setbacks or their current circumstances. No wonder they're never able to break free! They've forgotten their true identity.

The story of Edgar the eagle illustrates why you may need to have your mind renewed in order to see your calling as a believer. When Edgar was just a baby eagle, he fell off his family's high mountain ledge and landed among a flock of pigeons. The pigeons were friendly enough to take Edgar into their community and teach him how to live as one of them.

Edgar's education among the pigeons continued for more than a year. He flew along with them—never very high off the ground, of course—and scavenged for the meager food the pigeons ate.

But one day Edgar happened to see a huge eagle soaring effortlessly in the air, and something jumped in his heart. "Why can't *I* do that?" he asked the pigeons around him.

"Oh, you wouldn't want to fly that high," they warned him. "It's much too dangerous up there."

However, Edgar refused to be held back by his naysaying pigeon friends. When they weren't looking, he walked up the mountain until he came to the very perch he had fallen from as a baby. His mother eagle spotted him and joyfully welcomed him home. Soon he was soaring with her and the other eagles, far above the drab life of his pigeon friends.

You see, Edgar had the DNA of eagles, not pigeons. His DNA ultimately won out over his circumstances. For a time, he had been confused about his identity, living among the pigeons and seeing himself as one of them. He had accepted their lifestyle as his own, not realizing he was called to so much more.

Perhaps you find yourself living like a pigeon today—shallow, earthbound, purposeless. Maybe you've learned the lifestyle of those around you, even falling prey to sins and addictions that have dishonored God.

But as you read this story, I'm hopeful that God is reawakening something in your heart. You're longing to break out of your comfort zone and soar to new heights. (See Romans 12:2.) Like Edgar, you sense it's time to rediscover a high calling that had seemed a distant memory. If so, why not claim your destiny as an eagle?

If you're feeling weak and discouraged today, unable to get off the ground, I encourage you to meditate on this amazing promise from God:

Those who wait on the LORD
Shall renew their strength;
They shall mount up with wings like eagles,
They shall run and not be weary,
They shall walk and not faint.   (Isaiah 40:31)

He promises you new strength, new endurance, and new victory when you come into His presence and wait upon Him. So if you find yourself flapping like a pigeon instead of soaring like an eagle, it's time to break out of your frustrating circumstances. *It's time to fly!*

SIXTEEN

DELIVERED FROM LO DEBAR

Has life been unfair to you? Have you been crippled by circumstances beyond your control? If so, don't lose heart. There's a Bible story that should give you great hope for your future.

Mephibosheth's Misfortune

King David's friend Jonathan had a crippled son named Mephibosheth. When the boy was five years old, his nanny picked him and fled the palace at the news of Saul and Jonathan's death at Jezreel. But in her hurry to leave, she dropped Mephibosheth and he became lame in both feet. (See 2 Samuel 4:4.)

Think of how unfortunate and unfair this was. Sometimes we're crippled by our own dumb choices, but in this case Mephibosheth did nothing wrong. It was just a freak accident, yet it would impact him for the rest of his life.

Although it is still a tragedy when someone becomes crippled today, it was even worse during Old Testament times. Without wheelchairs, elevators, or cars, can you imagine how hard it would be for such a person to get around? He would be forever dependent on others—a situation that would rob anyone of dignity and hope.

Ironically, Mephibosheth's name meant "dispeller of shame" or "one who blows away shame." While that was his calling in the eyes of God, it took many years before this paralyzed man could break free from his shame and poor self-image.

The reason I love this story is that I can relate! Growing up in an inner-city culture of poverty, abuse, and addiction could have permanently crippled me. And the fact is, we've *all* been crippled, to one degree or another, by sin and the traumas of life. No one is exempt. Whether you're rich or poor, black or white, male or female, there's no way to pass through this life without being injured in some way. Even though relatively few people are *physically* crippled like Mephibosheth was, countless others have been crippled *emotionally* or *spiritually*.

But, praise God, He doesn't want to leave us hopeless or unfulfilled. As we'll see in a moment, the tragic beginning to Mephibosheth's story eventually becomes a beautiful illustration of redemption and restoration.

Brought Back to the Palace

Things began to turn around for Mephibosheth in 2 Samuel 9. King David started looking for descendants of Saul and Jonathan so that he could *"show him kindness"* to them for Jonathan's sake (verse 1). One of Saul's servants told the king about Jonathan's son, Mephibosheth, but it wasn't a pretty picture: in addition to being crippled in both feet, this bitter young man was living in a desolate place called Lo Debar. (See verses 3–4.)

Residing in Lo Debar would be like living in the worst imaginable slum today. The Hebrew word means "without pasture." It was a dry desert, where nothing much would grow…a desolate wilderness, where people lived isolated and unfruitful lives.

Worst of all, Lo Debar was on the *east* side of the Jordan River— outside of the Promised Land. In modern terminology, we might say that Mephibosheth was living "on the wrong side of the tracks."

Take a moment to pause and reflect on whether any of this applies to *your* life today. Are you still feeling paralyzed in some area of your life, such as your finances, career, health, relationships, or addictions? Do you find yourself dependent on the government or others for your livelihood, unable to stand on your own? And are you experiencing God's purpose and "Promised Land," or are you living in a dry and desolate place like Lo Debar?

When David heard about the deplorable circumstances of this son of Jonathan, he could have just ended the discussion. It would have been easy to conclude that Mephibosheth's situation was simply too big of a mess to remedy. But instead, David had the disabled man taken away from his squalor and brought to the palace in Jerusalem.

Friend, I don't know your situation today. Maybe you already have a wonderful life, with no real complaints. But perhaps you find yourself crippled in some way, paralyzed from believing God and achieving your true potential. If so, I want you to notice what happened here: David didn't give up on the man because of his pathetic living situation. In the same way, God hasn't given up on *you*!

Remember that Mephibosheth was crippled in *both* feet. This means he was unable to bring *himself* back to the palace in Jerusalem. He had to be *carried,* which is an accurate picture of God's amazing grace in our lives today. (See Ephesians 2:8–9.) He saved us when we were powerless to save ourselves. (See Romans 5:6–8.)

"I Will Restore You"

Mephibosheth was understandably apprehensive about *why* the king had summoned him. Was he, a potential threat to the throne of David, about to be killed by royal decree? David had to reassure him, *"Don't be afraid…for I will surely show you kindness for the sake of your father Jonathan. I will restore to you all the land that belonged to your grandfather Saul, and you will always eat at my table"* (2 Samuel 9:7 NIV).

This verse is packed full of important principles for those who are seeking to break free from some kind of toxic habit or situation. When you are trying to make some kind of major change in your life, fear will always be one of your biggest enemies and stumbling blocks. But God is saying to you, as David told this crippled man, *"Don't be afraid."* Why? Because He wants to *"show you kindness"* and transform your life.

Then David said one of the most beautiful phrases in the entire Bible: *"I will restore to you…."* That is God's message to you today, my friend! He wants to restore *everything* the enemy has stolen from you in the past.

Has your health been stolen? Your finances? Your marriage? Your kids? Your peace of mind? The Lord knows what the devil has taken from you, and He stands ready to restore those things when you cry out to Him and follow His instructions.

You Are Worthy!

But Mephibosheth faced another barrier in his heart, making it very difficult to receive what David was so generously offering him. He immediately protested that he was *unworthy* of such favor from the king.

Many of us have struggled with similar feelings when presented with God's incredible promises. It's not so much that we doubt the Lord, but we doubt our own merit and worthiness. God wants to set us free from guilt and shame, just as David did for Mephibosheth. So it's time to quit worrying about our shortcomings, remembering God's promise that *"There is therefore now no condemnation to those who are in Christ Jesus"* (Romans 8:1).

Even when Mephibosheth protested that he was unworthy, David *insisted* on showing him kindness and favor. As the chapter ends, we're told that this crippled son of Jonathan *"ate continually at the king's table"* (2 Samuel 9:13).

Just like Mephibosheth, *you* are called by God to be a prince or princess in the King's palace. Yes, you may have fallen, through your own fault or the failings of others. Yet while you may have felt unworthy of His favor, He wants to give it to you anyway.

Hear the Lord's amazing invitation today. He wants to restore what you've lost. He's beckoning you to dine at His table as one of His sons or daughters. And if you find yourself without strength, He'll even *carry you* there!

SEVENTEEN

DON'T JUST SIT THERE

Few things are as frustrating for preachers as running into folks who *say* they want to get unstuck from some toxic habit or situation, but who refuse to *do* anything to make that happen. I don't whether to laugh or cry when someone tells me, "Bishop Bloomer, I've decided to quit doing drugs...just not *today*."

You would be amazed to know how many people act as if God will transform their lives without any steps of obedience on their part. They complain that they don't have a job, but it's been weeks since they sent out a résumé. They say they want a better marriage, but are unwilling to go for counseling. They claim to sincerely want to kick an addiction, yet they refuse to go into rehab, join AA, or find a sponsor to hold them accountable.

The more I learn about God's ways, the more I appreciate the delicate partnership He expects between what He does and what we must do. The Christian life is a supernatural life: God provides the *super*, but we must provide the *natural*.

Saint Augustine, one of the early theologians of the church, is supposed to have said it this way: "Without God, we cannot. Without us, God will not." This means that you will never get where you need to go without God's help. But it *also* means God won't give you the help you need if you refuse to step out in faith to follow His instructions.

Four Lepers' Leap of Faith

This principle is vividly displayed in the story of four lepers sitting at the city gate during a time of famine. All around the city, the enemy army of Syrians were camped in siege, keeping any food from entering into the gates. The lepers' situation continued to go from bad to worse.

If these leprous men were like many people today, they would have just sat there and complained. "Why doesn't the government do something?" they might have said. Or else, "People should be more generous in giving us handouts."

But thankfully these men opted for a different approach. They asked themselves what *action* they could take to change their lot in life. *"Why are we sitting here until we die?"* they asked (2 Kings 7:3).

If you're trying to break loose from a bad situation, this is a profound question! If you just keep sitting in the same old spot, you'll eventually grow old and die! The Bible is full of stories of people who received amazing breakthroughs from God. But in nearly every case, they had to take some step of faith before their turnaround came.

These four lepers finally came up with a plan, and it was definitely a *risky* plan:

> *If we say, "We will enter the city," the famine is in the city, and we shall die there. And if we sit here, we die also. Now therefore, come, let us surrender to the army of the Syrians. If they keep us alive, we shall live; and if they kill us, we shall only die.*
>
> (verse 4)

These men clearly were desperate. They realized that they would surely die if they did nothing, and they also might die if they followed their plan to surrender to the Syrian army that was surrounding their city. But then and now, a powerful principle is demonstrated: *No risk, no reward.*

Not in their wildest imagination could the lepers have anticipated the blessings they were about to receive. They hoped for *survival*, and would have been content with that. But God wanted to give them so much more!

Friend, take a moment to assess what you're really expecting out of life from God. If you're just hoping for survival, barely scraping by, you need to set your sights much higher. The Lord wants to give you abundance far beyond your comprehension! (See Ephesians 3:20.)

The Risk Rewarded

The lepers rose at twilight to approach the Syrian camp, hoping for sanctuary. To their shock, no one was there!

> *The LORD had caused the army of the Syrians to hear the noise of chariots and the noise of horses—the noise of a great army; so they said to one another, "Look, the king of Israel has hired against us the kings of the Hittites and the kings of the Egyptians to attack us!" Therefore they arose and fled at twilight, and left the camp intact—their tents, their horses, and their donkeys— and they fled for their lives.* (2 Kings 7:6–7)

The lepers had not only broken loose from their dire poverty and lack, but they had also entered into a fantastic new level of prosperity. Walking into one of the tents, they ate and drank their fill—something that hadn't been possible for a long, long time. Then they carried away silver, gold, and clothing, and they found a place to hide it.

Up until now, the story is all about how you can get unstuck and experience a dramatic turnaround in your own life. By taking a small but risky step of faith, the lepers triggered a remarkable, unexpected outpouring of the blessings of God.

But friend, never forget: The abundant life is not just about you! Yes, your heavenly Father loves you and He wants to bless you. But once you are blessed, He wants you to *be* a blessing to others.

Although their initial inclination was to hoard the blessings they received from the Syrian camp, somehow these men were convicted of their selfishness:

> *Then they said to one another, "We are not doing right. This day is a day of good news, and we remain silent. If we wait until morning light, some punishment will come upon us. Now there- fore, come, let us go and tell the king's household." (2 Kings 7:9)*

Make no mistake about it: When God enables you to break loose from the things hindering you, it's *a day of good news.* You can't keep the blessings to yourself. Instead of remaining silent, you need to go and tell someone!

EIGHTEEN

FREED IN THE FURNACE

Usually we think of the trials of life as something we hope God will deliver us *from*. And indeed the Bible promises this: *"Many are the afflictions of the righteous, but the LORD delivers him out of them all"* (Psalm 34:19).

However, there's another side to this which we often overlook. Yes, God can deliver us from our trials. But more often, He delivers us *in* and *through* the trials of life. In other words, the Lord often uses our tests and afflictions to set us free from the things that bind us.

Let me share a story that illustrates this well.

Refusing to People-Please

In Daniel chapter 3, King Nebuchadnezzar made a huge golden image that everyone was commanded to bow down before. Three young Hebrew men—Shadrach, Meshach, and Abed-Nego— refused to worship the king's image, and they were thrown into the fiery furnace.

When throwing these men into the furnace, the king mocked them and asked, *"Who is the god who will deliver you from my hands?"* (verse 15). Shadrach, Meshach, and Abed-Nego answered:

Our God whom we serve is able to deliver us from the burning fiery furnace, and He will deliver us from your hand, O king. But if not, let it be known to you, O king, that we do not serve your gods, nor will we worship the gold image which you have set up.

(verses 17–18)

There's a lot of wisdom in this response. These men knew the Lord was *able* to deliver them from their fiery trial. But even if He didn't, they had resolved not to compromise their faith.

Pause to put yourself in their position. Would you be willing to bow down to the king's image in order to avoid the fiery furnace? Or what if machete-wielding ISIS warriors said they would cut off your head unless you renounced your devotion to Jesus Christ?

These young Jewish men weren't people-pleasers. They were committed to pleasing God rather than the king. They refused to squeeze into the mold of the surrounding culture—even if they had to pay with their lives.

I'm convinced that much of the bondage people suffer is because of people-pleasing. Wanting to fit in with the crowd, they foolishly get high, get drunk, or get laid. At the beginning, the compromises seem small, but if you give the devil an inch, he always takes a mile. There's an old maxim that says, "Sin starts as a cobweb, but soon becomes a cable."

The king was so infuriated at the response of the three men that he heated the furnace seven times hotter than usual. Perhaps it seems that way for you today. Like the young men in this story, you've tried to be faithful to God, but you find yourself in a fiery furnace nevertheless. If so, don't despair. The story isn't over yet!

The three men were in some serious "bondage" when they went into the fire: "*These men were bound in their coats, their trousers, their turbans, and their other garments, and were cast into the midst of the burning fiery furnace*" (Daniel 3:21). If this wasn't clear enough already, we're told that they "*fell down bound*" when they entered the fire (verse 23).

The Fire May Be Your Friend

Friend, you may not believe me, but I have a hunch that you were bound up in some way when you entered your season of fiery affliction. The bondage may have been obvious to all—something like an addiction. Or it may have been confined to the secret places of your heart—emotional bondage like fear, anger, loneliness, or depression. And while it's hard to believe while you're going through it, the fire may actually turn out to be your *friend*.

King Nebuchadnezzar looked into the furnace, expecting to see the burning flesh of the three young men who had defied him. Instead, he saw a quite astonishing sight. He asked those around him,

> *Did we not cast three men bound into the midst of the fire?...I see four men loose, walking in the midst of the fire; and they are not hurt, and the form of the fourth is like the Son of God.*
>
> (verses 24–25)

What an encouraging story this is! Will we sometime be thrown into the fire of affliction, even if we've done all we can to obey the Lord? Yes, indeed. However, just as these men experienced, the Son of God will be in the fire with us. He is Immanuel (see Matthew 1:23), and He has promised to never leave us or forsake us (see Hebrews 13:5).

The king's representatives were shocked when they saw *"these men on whose bodies the fire had no power; the hair of their head was not singed nor were their garments affected, and the smell of fire was not on them"* (Daniel 3:27). Notice that although God didn't spare them from the fire, the fire had no power to harm them. When they were delivered out of the furnace, they didn't even have the smell of fire on them!

I don't know what you've been through, my friend, nor do I know what you're going through today. Instead of a fiery furnace, you may have experienced the fires of bankruptcy, divorce, illness, depression, or addiction.

But I don't want you to miss my favorite part of this story. Not only did Shadrach, Meshach, and Abed-Nego get delivered from the furnace—they also were set free from everything that had bound them before being put in the fire! The fire burned their bondage, but it did not touch their bodies. Before they were freed from the furnace, God used the furnace to free them from everything else that was binding them.

That is God's intention for *you* as well. You can be confident that the fire isn't sent into your life to destroy you but to set you free!

As this chapter comes to a close, take a moment to meditate on this beautiful promise from God that He will be with you through the flood waters and fiery trials of life:

> *Fear not, for I have redeemed you;*
> *I have called you by your name;*
> *You are Mine.*
> *When you pass through the waters, I will be with you;*
> *And through the rivers, they shall not overflow you.*
> *When you walk through the fire, you shall not be burned,*
> *Nor shall the flame scorch you.*   (Isaiah 43:1–2)

You see, there's no need to fear the fires. After you've been tested, you will come out like pure gold—*free indeed.* (See Job 23:10; John 8:36.)

NINETEEN

FOLLOWING THE GREAT LIBERATOR

Jesus' earthly ministry was all about liberation. He wanted people to break loose from all the things keeping them from His best for their life.

When His ministry began, Jesus didn't waste any time laying out this "liberation" theme:

> So He came to Nazareth, where He had been brought up. And as His custom was, He went into the synagogue on the Sabbath day, and stood up to read. And He was handed the book of the prophet Isaiah. And when He had opened the book, He found the place where it was written:
>
> "The Spirit of the LORD is upon Me,
> Because He has anointed Me
> To preach the gospel to the poor;
> He has sent Me to heal the brokenhearted,
> To proclaim liberty to the captives
> And recovery of sight to the blind,
> To set at liberty those who are oppressed;
> To proclaim the acceptable year of the LORD." (Luke 4:16–19)

Lots of churches and preachers talk about the Holy Spirit, but few seem to have the kind of ministry Jesus is describing here. The Son of God came with a powerful anointing to bring the resources of heaven to earth. The poor would be set free from poverty...the brokenhearted would be healed...the spiritual captives would be set free...the blind would receive their sight...and the oppressed would be liberated. Oh, how we need more of this kind of power today!

Jesus was quoting from Isaiah 61:1–2, a popular Scripture passage that His hearers knew was describing the coming Messiah. It's stunning to see that not much has changed among humankind since these words were written. People *still* need to be healed and set free from various kinds of oppression.

The next two verses, Isaiah 61:2–4, are also incredibly relevant to our world today:

> *"To comfort all who mourn,*
> *To console those who mourn in Zion,*
> *To give them beauty for ashes,*
> *The oil of joy for mourning,*
> *The garment of praise for the spirit of heaviness;*
> *That they may be called trees of righteousness,*
> *The planting of the LORD, that He may be glorified."*
> *And they shall rebuild the old ruins,*
> *They shall raise up the former desolations,*
> *And they shall repair the ruined cities,*
> *The desolations of many generations.*

Take a moment to apply these wonderful words to your own life. Do you need to be comforted over some loss you've experienced? Has some area of your life turned to ashes, needing God to restore hope and beauty? Do you want to exchange your heaviness and depression for the oil of joy and the garment of praise?

The passage also speaks words of hope for our troubled cities today. In so many ways, our major urban areas are desolate and in ruins, and the devastation has been mounting for *"many generations."* But it's time for those of us who follow the Great Liberator to arise and bring healing and restoration to our communities. If Jesus has liberated us, He can use us to liberate others.

The Jewish rabbis of Jesus' day used to quote this same passage as if it was some faraway dream of a future world. But no one dared to make the claim Jesus was about to make:

> *Then He closed the book, and gave it back to the attendant and sat down. And the eyes of all who were in the synagogue were fixed on Him. And He began to say to them, "Today this Scripture is fulfilled in your hearing."*   (Luke 4:20–21)

I absolutely *love* this part of the story. I meet so many church folks who tell me about the glorious days of revival and healing many decades ago. And others spend all their time thinking about some future day when Jesus will come back and take them to heaven. All of that is good, but what about *today?*

The rabbis told endless stories about the miracles God did in Old Testament times, and they spoke glowingly about a future age when the Messiah would rule and reign. But they had nothing of substance to offer people in the *present tense!*

Think about your own life, my friend. Do you have a present-tense faith? The Bible is full of references to this:

> *Having promise of the life that **now** is....*   (1 Timothy 4:8)

> ***Today** if you will hear His voice....*
> (Psalm 95:7; Hebrews 3:7)

> ***Now** is the accepted time; behold, **now** is the day of salvation.*
> (2 Corinthians 6:2)

You see, if you're ever going to break loose from the things holding you back, you will need a *now* kind of faith. Yesterday's faith won't do. Tomorrow's faith hasn't arrived yet. You need a powerful anointing of the Spirit of God today to break every yoke and chain that has kept you from fulfilling your destiny.

So go ahead and identify the area of your life where you need the Great Liberator to set you free. He can heal your sick body or your broken heart. He can replace fear, loneliness, and depression with His incredible love, joy, and peace.

What are you waiting for? He offers you these things today! Cry out to Him and listen for His instructions. This can be your day of liberation, preparing you to set others free as well.

TWENTY

READY FOR A NEW BEGINNING?

The longer I live, the more I'm convinced that each us will need a fresh start at one point or another in our life. And for many of us, this kind of new beginning will be needed more than once!

It has always intrigued me to see people making New Year's resolutions. Losing weight...getting out of debt...rekindling romance in their marriage...spending more time with the Lord or their children—there are many different areas of life where people typically seek a new beginning at the time of a new year.

But what if you need to break loose from some negative situation and it's only the middle of the summer? Well, thankfully, you don't have to wait for New Year's Day to start your turnaround. As the old saying goes, "*Today* is the first day of the rest of your life!"

The Bible is filled with stories of people who received a new beginning from God. King David was among those who testified that the Lord had given him a fresh start, delivering him from "*a horrible pit*" filled with "*miry clay*" (Psalm 40:2):

> *He has put a new song in my mouth—*
> *Praise to our God;*
> *Many will see it and fear,*
> *And will trust in the LORD.* (verse 3)

If you feel like you're in "*a horrible pit*" today, be encouraged by the fact that David had been in one too. Yet God took him from out of the pit and the miry clay and put his feet on a rock. The result was a *"new song"* in David's mouth—just as the Lord wants to do for you and me.

Learning from the Woman at the Well

Sometimes our new beginning comes when we least expect it. For example, I love the account of the Samaritan woman who had a life-changing encounter with Jesus while drawing water from a well in the town of Sychar. (See John 4:1–42.)

This woman really needed a turnaround. She had already been married five times, and she now was living with a man who wasn't her husband. However, despite her sordid past, she was about to meet someone who could turn things around and give her a wonderful new future.

Because of her past choices, this woman was a social outcast. To avoid being seen, she came to the well at midday when it was so hot that no one else would be there. But to her surprise, someone was sitting by the well when she arrived. Not a Samaritan, but a Jew. Not a woman, as normally would come to draw water, but a man. And He was *already there*, as if to await her arrival.

It was Jesus, and *He met her right where she was…*

- He knew all about this woman's shame and brokenness, just as He knows about yours and mine.

- He knew she was working to get water that would soon leave her thirsty again.

- He saw behind her self-assured facade and knew she was hungry for spiritual truth.

- He knew she needed the kind of turnaround that only He could provide.

Just as for this Samaritan woman, a fresh start is available to *you,* my friend. But that means forgetting the past and allowing God to fill your heart with a *"new song"* of praise for His salvation. It means fixing your eyes on Jesus (see Hebrews 12:1–2) and pressing forward toward His high calling for your life (see Philippians 3:12–14).

One of the intriguing parts of the Samaritan woman's story is found when she told Jesus, "*I know that Messiah is coming.... When He comes, He will tell us all things*" (John 4:25).

You see, this woman expected the Messiah to come *someday.* She could envision a future day when the Messiah would "*tell us all things.*"

However, she didn't recognize that her new beginning was *at hand.* There was no need to delay any longer. The long-awaited Messiah was standing *right next to her!* To the woman's amazement, Jesus told her, "*I who speak to you am He*" (verse 26).

Friend, there's a vital lesson here. Perhaps you've gotten used to thinking that your turnaround will come at some distant time in the future, if it ever comes at all. But Jesus the Messiah is not some faraway person. *He's right there with you,* just as He was for the Samaritan woman!

Ripple Effect

The woman from Samaria was transformed by her encounter with Jesus, but the story doesn't end there. Her transformation caused a ripple effect that impacted countless other lives as well: "*Many of the Samaritans of that city believed in Him because of the word of the woman who testified*" (verse 39).

This incredible impact was possible because a woman who had made numerous mistakes along the way came face-to-face with Jesus, the Messiah. In the same way, God wants to set *you* free from past frustrations, giving you a new life of fulfillment and impact.

You may not need the kind of forgiveness and restoration Jesus gave the woman at the well. Whatever your needs may be, I'm convinced God wants to give you supernatural breakthroughs, enabling you to break loose from everything that has held you back. Regardless of your struggles in the past, a better day is ahead. As Jesus told one of His disciples, "*You will see **greater things** than these*" (John 1:50).

Today, recognize Jesus' presence with you—wherever you may be in your life. In Him, you are a *"new creation,"* and *"all things have become new"* (2 Corinthians 5:17)!

TWENTY-ONE

LEAVE YOUR PAST BEHIND

You've probably met people who love to live in the past. Day after day, they nurse old wounds and relive past tragedies. They recall in great detail every time they were maligned and mistreated.

Often these people struggle to find intimacy because they're haunted by memories of trusted people who abused them. It's hard for them to trust God, because they recall a prayer made twenty years ago He didn't seem to answer. And often they find it hard to participate in a church, because they can't get over the hypocrisies of other Christians.

What do you say to people who are so bound by the heartaches of their yesterdays that they miss God's great plans for their life today? How can they shake off the shackles of the past? What can they do to experience a turnaround in their relationship with the Lord, so they can recover their joy and fulfill the divine purpose for their lives?

A Moment of Realization

The life of the Prodigal Son reached a turning point when he *"came to himself"* while feeding pigs (Luke 15:17). It took a while, but he finally realized he was reaping the bitter fruit of his poor choices. He knew if he stayed on his current path, his life would surely continue its downhill slide.

Until people come to this moment of realization, they will continue to wallow in the pigpen of yesterday's faults, failures, and hurts. The turning point can't come until they're truly desperate enough to *turn* and go in a new direction.

You may be saying, "Bishop Bloomer, I really *want* a new beginning, but I'm still troubled with past sins and failures, and with all the hurts and heartaches I've suffered." If the devil is taunting you with such things, I have great news for you: God can get you out of the enemy's pigpen of failure and despair!

Look at these encouraging promises from the book of Isaiah:

> *"Behold, the former things have come to pass,*
> *Now I declare new things;*
> *Before they spring forth I proclaim them to you."*
> *Sing to the* LORD *a new song,*
> *Sing His praise from the end of the earth!*
>
> (Isaiah 42:9–10 NASB)

> *Do not call to mind the former things,*
> *Or ponder things of the past.*
> *Behold, I will do something new,*
> *Now it will spring forth;*
> *Will you not be aware of it?*
> *I will even make a roadway in the wilderness,*
> *Rivers in the desert.*   (Isaiah 43:18–19 NASB)

Some powerful principles are contained in these brief passages of Scripture:

1. God declares His desire to give us a fresh start when we need a breakthrough.

2. He desires to give us a *"new song,"* so we can *"sing His praise from the end of the earth."*

3. He wants to stir our hearts to be *"aware"* of the new things He's doing in our lives.

4. We are told to not *"call to mind"* or *"ponder things of the past."*

5. No matter what kinds of difficult seasons we've been facing, God wants to *"make a roadway in the wilderness, rivers in the desert."*

I encourage you to spend some time meditating on these wonderful promises from God. Instead of the devil's *pigpen*, He wants to show you His *purpose* and *provision*.

The apostle Paul challenges us to turn our back on the past and then press onward toward our high calling in Christ: *"One thing I do: forgetting what lies behind and straining forward to what lies ahead"* (Philippians 3:13 ESV).

There are several important reasons why you need to forget the past:

+ God has told you to leave it behind.

+ You cannot change any part of it.

+ If you've asked God to forgive you and give you a new beginning, your past sins are forgotten.

+ God tells you to forgive anyone who has sinned against you, and you can't be fully released from your past until you release others.

Why worry or fret over something you cannot possibly control? Your past is finished, and there's nothing you can do to resurrect it. So bury it and let it stay dead!

Micah's Prayer

When you repent of your sins, forgive others, and ask God for a breakthrough or new beginning, He forgives and forgets your past misdeeds. Look at what the prophet Micah says about how God handles your sins and your past:

> *Who is a God like You, who pardons iniquity*
> *And passes over the rebellious act of the remnant*
> *of His possession?*
> *He does not retain His anger forever,*
> *Because He delights in unchanging love.*
> *He will again have compassion on us;*
> *He will tread our iniquities under foot.*
> *Yes, You will cast all their sins*
> *Into the depths of the sea.*   (Micah 7:18–19 NASB)

When the Lord forgives you, the Bible says He buries your sins in the deepest part of the ocean! As I heard someone say once, God then hangs a "No Fishing" sign to keep us from resurrecting those things ever again.

And notice the word "all": "You will cast *all* their sins into the depths of sea." Not one of your sins is so terrible that it's unforgivable. All of your sins were included when you asked Jesus Christ to come into your life...when you asked Him to forgive your sins and make you a child of God.

David's Prayer

Like Micah, King David declares that God "*pardons all your iniquities*" (Psalm 103:3 NASB). At one point in his life, David was under a cloud of shame after committing adultery and murder. Desperately needing a breakthrough of God's grace and mercy, He cried out for forgiveness and restoration:

> Create in me a clean heart, O God,
> And renew a steadfast spirit within me.
> Do not cast me away from Your presence,
> And do not take Your Holy Spirit from me.
> Restore to me the joy of Your salvation
> And uphold me by Your generous Spirit.   (Psalm 51:10–12)

It's clear that David doesn't want to settle for anything less than *full restoration*. He knew he needed a fresh start, as *The Message* translation brings out here:

> God, make a fresh start in me, shape a Genesis week from the chaos of my life. Don't throw me out with the trash, or fail to breathe holiness in me. Bring me back from gray exile, put a fresh wind in my sails!

My friend, God heard David's prayer—and He will hear *yours* as well. No matter what kind of pit you have dug for yourself, the Lord can forgive you and give you a fresh start.

How fantastic it is to go from a life of sin and death to a life of joy and peace! In another prayer, David testified of God's amazing grace:

> How blessed is he whose transgression is forgiven,
> Whose sin is covered!
> How blessed is the man to whom the LORD does not impute
> iniquity,
> And in whose spirit there is no deceit!...
> I acknowledged my sin to You,
> And my iniquity I did not hide;
> I said, "I will confess my transgressions to the LORD";
> And You forgave the guilt of my sin.   (Psalm 32:1–2, 5 NASB)

> As far as the east is from the west,
> So far has He removed our transgressions from us.
>   (Psalm 103:12 NASB)

Your past sins—*all* of them—have been covered by the blood of Jesus. Now it's time for you to forget them and leave them in the past, so your turnaround can begin!

TWENTY-TWO

FREED FROM SIN AND SHAME

Although God is intent on setting you free from *every* area of bondage in your life, the starting place is usually the issue of forgiveness.

One day Jesus was teaching to a packed house of people in Capernaum. Four men heard He was in town and carried their paralyzed friend to the meeting, hoping Jesus would heal him. (See Mark 2:1–12). But when they got there, things were more difficult than they expected. There was such a large crowd that they couldn't even get in the door, let alone carry a stretcher in.

More than Physical Healing

There's a powerful principle for us embedded in what happened next. These four men wouldn't let anything stop them in their mission. They climbed up on the roof, dug a hole, and lowered their crippled friend to Jesus.

Wow. What dedication! I love how the Bible says *"they had broken through"* (verse 4). This is a great illustration of the kind of perseverance we sometimes will need in order to receive our breakthrough from God. We may need to *climb higher* and *do some digging*!

But at this point the story takes an unexpected turn. The paralytic and his friends had come to this meeting to receive a physical healing, but Jesus said instead, *"Son, your sins are forgiven you"* (verse 5).

Do you see how puzzling this must have been? They probably wanted to reply, "Jesus, don't you get it? We didn't bring this man all the way here and then dig a hole on the roof of the house just to hear about forgiveness!"

But what they couldn't grasp was that forgiveness was the initial key to unlock *everything else* this man needed. Jesus *first* set him free from his sins, and *then* He released him from his sickness and paralysis:

> *"Which is easier, to say to the paralytic, 'Your sins are forgiven you,' or to say, 'Arise, take up your bed and walk'? But that you may know that the Son of Man has power on earth to forgive sins"—He said to the paralytic, "I say to you, arise, take up your bed, and go to your house." Immediately he arose, took up the bed, and went out in the presence of them all, so that all were amazed and glorified God, saying, "We never saw anything like this!"*   (verses 9–12)

Get Out of Jail Free

What a fantastic illustration that Jesus wants to break *every* chain in our lives. This is a theme throughout God's Word, and all of it is connected to what Jesus did for us on the cross:

> *Surely He has borne our griefs*
> *And carried our sorrows;*
> *Yet we esteemed Him stricken,*
> *Smitten by God, and afflicted.*
> *But He was wounded for our transgressions,*
> *He was bruised for our iniquities;*
> *The chastisement for our peace was upon Him,*
> *And by His stripes we are healed.*   (Isaiah 53:4–5)

In this brief passage foretelling Jesus' death on Calvary, it mentions some of the things His death liberated us from: griefs...sorrows...transgressions...and iniquities. And as a result, we received His peace and healing power as well.

Before moving too quickly to all the other ways you need Jesus to set you free, make sure you've stopped at the cross to receive His pardon from guilt and deliverance from shame. Every other type of liberation begins with that.

If you've ever played the popular board game *Monopoly*, you've probably received a "Get Out of Jail Free" card. Instead of trying to pay your way out of jail, that single card is your ticket to instant freedom.

Although many believers don't realize it, God has given *each* of us a "Get Out of Jail Free" card. Jesus' death on the cross makes it possible for us to escape from our prison of sin and death. People may try all sorts of other things to help them overcome their feelings of shame and condemnation, but only Jesus' blood can truly cleanse our sins and set us free.

If God has forgiven your shortcomings and sins, why should you remember them? If the devil keeps sowing condemnation in your life by bringing up your painful or sinful past, remember this: The devil is a liar! God's Word says, *"There is therefore now no condemnation to those who are in Christ Jesus"* (Romans 8:1)!

On the cross, Jesus bore all your fears, guilt, and shame…so you don't have to bear them any longer! Once you grasp this truth, you will not only be set free from the "jailhouse" of your past, but also free to go forward in God and experience a new beginning in Him.

What a blessing to receive God's "Get Out of Jail Free" card! So toss out any guilt, fear, shame, or condemnation, and come into God's presence with praise and worship on your lips.

From cover to cover, the message of the Bible is clear: God loves you and offers you total and complete forgiveness, deliverance from guilt and shame, and everything else as a bonus!

TWENTY-THREE

LOOSED FROM OLD-TIME RELIGION

I'll admit, I have mixed feelings when I hear people talk about getting back to the "old-time religion." You see, I've met some "religious" folks who don't look much like Jesus. They seem more like old-time *legalists* than old-time saints. They may tell people that salvation comes through the unmerited grace of God, but then they burden them down with crazy religious rules as soon as soon as they enter the church doors.

I know what I'm talking about. I grew up in a legalistic church where the women all wore long dresses and had their hair up in buns. They weren't allowed to wear jewelry, wear pants, or use makeup. And they always kept their heads covered in church.

To tell you the truth, they all looked *miserable* most of the time. And I was miserable too. If this was what it was like to truly follow Jesus, I decided I wanted no part of it. I wanted to break free!

Discard Religious Hypocrisy

Fortunately, I eventually met the real Jesus. I was relieved to discover that He was nothing like the legalists who were so proud of their religiosity and so condescending toward others who didn't dress like them or share their narrow views.

Jesus made it clear that *love* and *unity* would be the earmarks of His followers. (See John 13:34–35; John 17:20–23.) We just don't see enough of that in the church today. The church needs a radical spiritual awakening, making us lovers rather than haters, problem-solvers rather than mere critics. As Abraham Lincoln once said, "He has a right to criticize, who has a heart to help."

And when it comes to true religion, we're sorely misguided if we think that means carrying a big Bible, attending church with all our Christian friends, and saying "Praise the Lord!" all the time. Instead, we're told, *"Pure and genuine religion in the sight of God the Father means caring for orphans and widows in their distress and refusing to let the world corrupt you"* (James 1:27 NLT).

So I'm totally in favor of going back to the old-time religion if it means loving Jesus enough to care for orphans, widows, and other people in distress. Any other kind of spirituality is *false* religion, putting people in bondage rather than setting them free.

You've probably run into smug religious people who claim to represent God. Don't let them keep you from breaking loose from the bondage in your life!

The Pharisees portrayed themselves as guardians of the truths of the Scriptures, but Jesus saw them quite differently:

> *They crush people with unbearable religious demands and never lift a finger to ease the burden.... "For you are like whitewashed tombs—beautiful on the outside but filled on the inside with dead people's bones and all sorts of impurity. ...filled with hypocrisy and lawlessness."* (Matthew 23:4, 27–28 NLT)

If we are going to successfully challenge our society on the moral issues of our day, we must do some housecleaning at home. We must regain true spirituality—to make us more like Jesus—and discard religious hypocrisy that has made us too much like the Pharisees.

Isaiah's Vision for Transformation

Although I consider myself an evangelical, I'm not always on board with how things are done in some evangelical churches. We've done a pretty good job of preaching on John 3:16 and the need for an individual to be born again, and that is a crucial starting point. But if our religion is genuine, it will bear fruit not only in changing our own lives, but also our families and our communities. Transformation starts with the salvation of a soul, but God then wants to work through that soul to save families, churches, communities and even nations.

Remember what I shared earlier about Jesus' first recorded teaching? His keynote address based on Isaiah 61 provided a fitting preamble to His anointed earthly ministry *"to bring good news to the poor…comfort the brokenhearted…proclaim that captives will be released and prisoners will be freed."* He was telling *"those who mourn that the time of the LORD's favor has come"* (Isaiah 61:1–2 NLT).

Isn't that wonderful news, even today? There are *still* countless people who are poor, brokenhearted, and in need of comfort. There are *still* multitudes of people imprisoned by sin, addictions, toxic relationships, fear, and depression, desperately in need of deliverance.

Jesus came to help people like this—people like you and me. Instead of allowing us to languish on the ash heap, He offers us *"a crown of beauty"* and *"a joyous blessing."* He wants to replace our anxiety and despair with *"festive praise."* And instead of leaving us like hapless trees blown over by the circumstances of life, He wants to make *"great oaks…planted for his own glory"* (verse 3 NLT).

Isaiah 61 is a beautiful passage, and I have heard many excellent sermons on how God can transform a person's life through the "great exchange" described there. However, it's important not to forget the rest of the chapter. The good news presented in Isaiah 61 extends past individual salvation to the transformation of entire communities and cities.

Those whose lives are changed by God's grace are given a powerful mission to fulfill: *"They will rebuild the ancient ruins, repairing cities destroyed long ago. They will revive them, though they have been deserted for many generations"* (verse 4 NLT).

Read that again and let it really sink in. If you are a child of God, He has commissioned you to *"rebuild the ancient ruins, repairing cities."* Do you know any cities that need to be rebuilt and repaired today? Of course you do. Places like Detroit, Oakland, Baltimore, and Ferguson may be in the news, but it's a good bet that *your* city needs some repairs as well.

It's time for the urban churches to lead a turnaround in their communities. We need to throw off our feelings of defeat and victim-hood, instead embracing what God's Word says about us:

> *Instead of shame and dishonor, you will enjoy a double share of honor. You will possess a double portion of prosperity in your land, and everlasting joy will be yours.... I will faithfully reward my people for their suffering and make an everlasting covenant with them.... Their descendants will be recognized and honored among the nations. Everyone will realize that they are a people the* Lord *has blessed."*   (verses 7–9 NLT)

You are called to be a victor instead of a victim. Instead of being bullied by the world and squeezed into its mold, you are called to be salt and light, bringing hope and transformation in the name of Jesus. God wants to set you free—not just for your own sake, but so you can make a positive impact on your community.

TWENTY-FOUR

FREED FROM TORMENT

There are lots of ways the devil can bring a person into bondage, but often it begins when they harbor unforgiveness. Some Bible teachers even refer to unforgiveness as "the bait of Satan," since *nothing* invites Satan's activity in our life more certainly than that. In contrast, extending grace and forgiveness to others is a powerful key to unlock our *own* prison doors.

Earlier, I described how we've been given a "Get Out of Jail Free" card through the blood of Jesus shed on the cross. But it breaks God's heart that many of His children have gone *back* to "jail." (See Matthew 23:37.) He has graciously forgiven their sins, but they've allowed unforgiveness toward others to bring them back into a spiritual prison.

In Matthew 18:21–35, Jesus tells a sobering story about a man who was forgiven a huge debt. The man had come before his master to plead for mercy, and the master was gracious to him: "*The master of that servant was moved with compassion, released him, and forgave him the debt*" (verse 27).

Friend, this is exactly what the Lord has done for you in Jesus' death on the cross:

+ He showed His compassion for you.

+ He forgave your debt of sin.

+ He released you from the prison of your past.

Unfortunately, though, the story doesn't have a happy ending. This man who received such mercy then refused to forgive someone who owed him a very small debt:

That servant went out and found one of his fellow servants who owed him a hundred denarii; and he laid hands on him and took him by the throat, saying, "Pay me what you owe!" So his fellow servant fell down at his feet and begged him, saying, "Have patience with me, and I will pay you all." And he would not, but went and threw him into prison till he should pay the debt.

(verses 28–30)

Notice that forgiving others is a *choice*, not a feeling. When asked for mercy, he was *unwilling* to give it. Although he had been set free from his own debt, he chose to put the other man in prison.

However, the master of the first servant was irate when he heard about the situation:

Then his master, after he had called him, said to him, "You wicked servant! I forgave you all that debt because you begged me. Should you not also have had compassion on your fellow servant, just as I had pity on you?" (verses 32–33)

The master's anger resulted in terrible consequences for the man who refused to forgive: *"His master...delivered him to the **torturers** until he should pay all that was due to him"* (verse 34).

Jesus ends this story with a pointed warning about the consequences of unforgiveness: *"So My heavenly Father also will do to you if each of you, from his heart, does not forgive his brother his trespasses"* (verse 35).

Notice this sobering truth: Those who hold on to unforgiveness will be handed over to *"torturers."* Other translations say *"tormentors"* (KJV) or *"jailers"* (NIV).

Of course, this isn't God's will for our lives! Jesus died to set us *free* from the jailhouse of guilt, shame, and torment. But our unwillingness to forgive others will bring us back into a prison of our own making. The "Get Out of Jail Free" card will only work when we've forgiven those who have wronged us.

Jesus' story is an illustration of a warning He also gave in the Sermon on the Mount. After instructing us to pray *"Forgive us our debts, as we forgive our debtors"* (Matthew 6:12), Jesus added, *"For if you forgive others for their transgressions, your heavenly Father will also forgive you. But if you do not forgive others, then your Father will not forgive your transgressions"* (verses 14–15 NASB).

Many people today are being tormented by their past, their failures and mistakes, or the ways they've been victimized by another person. Sometimes the past traumas are very real, very severe, and very painful. Perhaps you've been victimized by an abusive relationship, a cheating spouse, or a dishonest business partner. If so, God wants to wrap His love and compassion around you today—yet He still requires you to forgive the person who wronged you.

If you find yourself in a place of torment today, God wants to release you. But the key to your prison is in your *own* hand. I encourage you today to get away for some time with God, asking Him to work His forgiveness in your heart.

As long as it takes, spend time choosing to forgive each and every person who has hurt you. Tear up every "IOU," and release them from their debts. The person ultimately set free will be *you*!

TWENTY-FIVE

OVERCOMING OFFENSES

No one said it was *easy* to forgive others. It's especially hard if you've been hurt deeply and if you've been holding on to your offenses for a long time. We've all had times when we feel justified in holding an angry grudge against someone. "They just don't *deserve* to be forgiven!" we tell the Lord.

Of course, *we* didn't deserve to be forgiven either. Yet He freely and willingly pardoned us through His grace and mercy. He didn't wait for us to clean up our act first, but rather declared us "Not guilty!" when we were still His enemies, living in sin. (See Romans 5:1–8.)

Biblical Examples of Forgiveness

If you are struggling to let go of offenses toward other people, here are two important things you must remember: 1) The main person hurt by your offense is not the other person, it's *you!* 2) As severely as you have been wronged, your trauma is no greater than was experienced by many men and women of God in the Bible.

- Because of the jealousy of his brothers, **Joseph** was thrown into the bottom of a well, became a slave in Egypt, and spent years in a dungeon. Yet he chose to forgive his brothers and welcome them into the prosperity God had given him. Instead of taking revenge against his brothers, Joseph told them, *"You meant evil against me, but God meant it for good"* (Genesis 50:20).

- **Job** found a wonderful reversal of his fortunes when he prayed for his friends—even though they had spent many days badgering and criticizing him. (See Job 42:10–12.)

- The **Samaritan woman at the well** (see John 4:1–42) and the **woman caught in adultery** (see John 8:1–11) both endured trauma at the hands of men and because of their own foolish choices—but they each received a new beginning when Jesus forgave and restored them.

- **Stephen** forgave those who were stoning him to death: *"Lord, do not hold this sin against them!"* (Acts 7:60 NASB). This act of forgiveness was one of the primary factors leading to the conversion of the apostle Paul.

- **Jesus**, while carrying the sins of the world on His back on the cross, issued a powerful word of forgiveness that has echoed down through the centuries: *"Father, forgive them; for they do not know what they are doing"* (Luke 23:34 NASB).

So remember this when you're tempted to throw yourself a pity party and hold on to offenses toward others: God wants you to follow the example of Jesus and these other leaders. Don't delay. Your own freedom will begin when you freely forgive those who have treated you unjustly.

Yes, forgiveness often is very difficult. But it's an essential key to your new beginning. David prayed, *"Search me, O God, and know my heart; try me and know my anxious thoughts; and see if there be any **hurtful way** in me"* (Psalm 139:23–24 NASB). Make no mistake about it: Unforgiveness is a *"hurtful way"* that will imprison you with torment unless you deal with it.

Don't just *assume* you've forgiven people who have hurt you. You may need to spend some time asking God to search your heart. If you're still *talking about* the offense—months or even years after it occurred—it's likely that you still have some forgiving to do. Friend, take time today to allow the Lord to search your heart and remove any *"hurtful way"* or unforgiveness that is keeping you imprisoned to your past.

Don't Hold On to Offense

If you're still struggling with this, perhaps this story will help:

A mother baked some chocolate chip cookies for her young son. "Tommy," she told him, "I'm putting the cookies in the cookie jar. You're not allowed to eat any now, but you can have some after dinner."

Of course, Tommy couldn't wait for this special treat. While his mom was in the other room, Tommy opened the cookie jar and reached in to grab a few big cookies. However, when he tried to remove his hand, he discovered that it was stuck.

Tommy began to cry and then screamed to his mom, "HELP! I'M TRAPPED!"

When Tommy's mom ran into the room, she saw that his hand was stuck, and he was sobbing hysterically. She decided the only option was to break open the cookie jar so he could get his hand out. When she broke the jar, Tommy's mom was shocked to discover he was still clutching three cookies in his little hand. "Tommy, why didn't you *let go* of the cookies?" she asked in amazement.

"Because I *wanted* them!" Tommy replied as he broke into tears again.

If you find yourself stuck and in some kind of bondage to the enemy today, you may need to let go of some "cookies" you're holding on to. God wants to set you free from anything that has hindered you from fulfilling His highest purposes—but you need to *let go*.

Like Tommy, you may be tempted to protest that the cookies you're grasping are something desirable and *good*—not something negative. But remember that *anything* is negative if it keeps us from God's *best* for our life. Paul says, **"Whatever** things were gain to me, those things I have **counted as loss** for the sake of Christ" (Philippians 3:7).

Today God offers you a fresh start, but you must let go of anything holding you back from your spiritual freedom in Jesus Christ. Once your surrender is complete, you'll be amazed by how quickly your new beginning comes into view and God gives you long-awaited breakthroughs through prayer.

So go ahead and thank God for His plan to set you free. Since He has so graciously forgiven you, you are now able to forgive those who have caused you pain. Take time to go through the list of those who have hurt you, and forgive them, one by one, for what they did to cause you pain. As you do, repent of any anger, bitterness, or desire for revenge that may still be in your heart.

Today and in the days ahead, when the enemy tries to remind you of these past hurts, remind *him* that you have chosen to forgive these people as God has forgiven you. With His amazing peace in your heart, you'll be able to stand in complete victory in Jesus' name!

TWENTY-SIX

THE CURE FOR BITTERNESS

A friend recently told me two observations he had while attending a reunion of old friends he hadn't seen in many years.

His first observation was that virtually *everyone* had dealt with some kind of crisis or loss in the years since he had last seen them. A few had gone through a health crisis, such as a heart attack or kidney failure. Others were grieving over lost loved ones or downturns in their career. And several had experienced the pain of divorce or difficulties with their children.

This first observation was a great reminder that we all "go through stuff" in life. No one is exempt. Your trials may be different from mine, but we're all in the same boat when it comes to *having* difficult experiences.

However, my friend's second observation was even more eye-opening: While everyone had gone through adversity of one kind or another, their reactions and outcomes were entirely different. Adversity had caused some of his friends to become *bitter,* and had caused others to become *better.*

Bitter or Better?

This same principle is seen in nature, where fire causes completely different outcomes in the elements it touches. When *wood* is placed in the fire, it turns to *ashes.* Yet when *gold* is placed in the fire, it's refined into *purer gold.* The fire doesn't determine the outcome, but simply reveals the character of what it touches.

Of course, people aren't inanimate objects like wood or gold. We've been given free will, the power to *choose* our attitudes and responses to the events we face in life. That's why two people can experience exactly the same kind of trauma, with totally different outcomes. It all depends on their choices and their character.

I'm intrigued by how God turned things around for many Bible heroes who experienced hardships or losses.

Naomi

Naomi, for example, recognized that her losses had made her bitter, and she even wanted her friends to call her by the new name: "Bitter." (See Ruth 1:20.) I admire Naomi for this because few people are that self-aware or honest about their condition. Bitter people seldom seem to realize the seriousness of their malady.

It is also very encouraging that Naomi's friends were determined to see the best in her, and they never called her by the unflattering label she had chosen for herself. Instead, they continued to call her *Naomi*, which means "sweet" or "pleasant."

I hope *you* have friends like that. There is no greater asset if you need to get unstuck and make the journey from *bitter* to *better*.

Fortunately, by the end of Naomi's story, both her *heart* and her *circumstances* had changed in a positive way. Although she admittedly had been bitter at certain points in her journey through life, she didn't *stay* that way.

The Israelites

The Israelites had to overcome bitterness in their journey through the wilderness. God had mightily delivered them from Egypt and set them on a pathway to the Promised Land. When their progress was blocked by the Red Sea, He miraculously parted the waters and then vanquished Pharaoh's army.

So far, so good. But after the Israelites' triumph over the Egyptians at the Red Sea, they faced a trial of another kind:

> *Moses brought Israel from the Red Sea…. And they went three days in the **wilderness** and found **no water**. Now when they came to Marah, they could not drink the waters of Marah, for they were **bitter**. Therefore the name of it was called Marah. And the people complained against Moses, saying, "What shall we drink?" So he cried out to the LORD, and the LORD showed him a **tree**. When he **cast it** into the waters, **the waters were made sweet**…. Then they came to **Elim**, where there were **twelve wells of water** and seventy palm trees; so they camped there by the waters.* (Exodus 15:22–25, 27)

What a fascinating story. God had miraculously enabled His people to escape from captivity in Egypt, yet then they found themselves in a desolate wilderness, where there was no water. Finally, they discovered abundant water at Marah—but the water was *bitter*.

Maybe you've found yourself in a similar place. Despite your sincere attempts to follow God's leading, you've sometimes ended up in a barren spiritual desert. And right when you think there's some hope, the water turns out to be bitter.

We've gone through some tough economic times in recent years, and many believers have had their faith and their relationships severely tested. They feel frustrated at themselves, their boss (if they still have a boss), their spouse, their church, and perhaps toward the entire Christian life. For many, it has been a baffling season. Whatever happened to the abundant, joy-filled life the Bible promises us?

The truth is, we've all encountered the bitter waters of Marah at one time or another. However, there's good news in this remarkable account: *Bitter waters can be turned sweet!*

The Cross and Bitterness

So how can this transformation occur? By applying the cross (the tree) to the situation. This requires something more than passive doctrinal assent, however. Yes, *"the LORD showed [Moses] a tree,"* but nothing significant happened until *"he cast it into the waters"* (verse 25).

When applied by faith, the cross provides *everything we need* to reverse our toxic situations and bitter attitudes. Through the cross...

+ We receive forgiveness from God and are reconciled into an intimate relationship with Him.

+ We forgive each other, as He has forgiven us.

+ We die to ourselves, making it possible to obey God and serve others.

+ We see our unfair and toxic circumstances from the vantage point of God's love and His ability to triumph over evil with good.

Perhaps you're saying in your heart at this point, "But Bishop Bloomer, what if I'm the only one trying to apply the cross to a toxic situation? How can it possibly work if everyone else isn't on board?"

Well, you are partially correct. You might not be able to transform *everything* around you into an oasis of sweet waters. Yet whenever you touch the bitter waters you face with the power of the cross, two things automatically happen: Your *own* attitudes change, and God is free to bring transformation to others around you as well.

However, remember this, my friend: *If you've been waiting for God to turn your bitter waters sweet, He may be waiting for you to embrace the cross and apply it to your circumstances.* And instead of waiting for someone else to initiate the healing process, you may need to take the first step. Are you ready?

This story ends with an incredible message of encouragement. When you embrace the cross and die to yourself, you'll soon be transported from a desert wilderness to a whole new land of blessing—to *"Elim, where there were twelve wells of water and seventy palm trees"* (verse 27).

Isn't it great to know that bitter people—whether Naomi, the Israelites, or you and I—can break free and move toward *better attitudes* and *better days?* No matter what we've gone through in the past or are going through today, we can entrust our lives to the Lord, our faithful Creator and Provider. (See 1 Peter 4:19.) And no matter how hard our hearts have become, we can ask Him to soften them so we don't remain captives to bitterness.

Sadly, there is also a warning here. Even though many Bible characters experienced a joyful new beginning when they got unstuck from their bitterness, others never learned the keys of going from bitter to better. For example, Esau never recovered from the *"root of bitterness"* that had become entrenched in his heart (Hebrews 12:15).

I hope you haven't allowed life's traumas and losses to make you hardhearted, cynical, or bitter. But if you have, there's still time for a turnaround. The poison of bitterness can be replaced by its antidote—grace and forgiveness, through the power of the cross.

So drop the excuses for your bad attitudes. If you'll let Him, God stands ready to give you a heart transplant, and that will eventually transform your circumstances too.

TWENTY-SEVEN

OVERCOMING FAILURE

Failure is something we've all experienced at one time or another. Sometimes the failure is pretty insignificant: a poor grade on a test, striking out on our little league baseball team, or flunking our first driving test. But other failures are a lot more painful: a lost job, a divorce, rebellious children, financial ruin.

The only people who never fail are those who never attempt anything! And throughout history, the people with the greatest success stories were those who had to learn to bounce back from great disappointments and failures.

Every Hero Fails

Babe Ruth is famous for hitting *714 home runs* in his amazing baseball career, but few people remember that he also *struck out 1,330 times*, almost twice as often. If you want to hit a lot of home runs in life, you can't be afraid to strike out from time to time. If Babe Ruth had spent time thinking about all his strikeouts, he would have become too discouraged to be the great ballplayer that he was.

Basketball legend Michael Jordan said on a TV commercial toward the end of his NBA career: "I've missed more than 9,000 shots in my career. I've lost more than 300 games. Twenty-six times I've been trusted to take the game-winning shot—and missed. I've failed over and over and over again in my life, and that is why I succeed."

Should we consider Michael Jordan a failure at basketball because he missed a lot of shots and lost a lot of games? Of course not. Yet missing the winning shot in a big game would have sent some players into a tailspin. They might have gone into a slump for several games, unable to shake the memory of their failure. But not Michael. He learned to start each game with a clean slate.

Michael Jordan had actually learned to overcome failure several years before starting his career in the NBA. In 1978 he was cut from the basketball team at Laney High School in Wilmington, North Carolina. Instead of giving up, he worked hard to improve his game. He made the team the following year, and by 1985 he was the NBA rookie of the year.

Without exception, every successful leader in history experienced ridicule, defeat, and discouragement at one time or another. Christopher Columbus, Galileo, Copernicus, Alexander Graham Bell, Abraham Lincoln, Thomas Edison, the Wright Brothers, and many other great pioneers in their respective fields endured numerous failures and frequent rejection.

The Bible is very candid about the failures of its heroes. Although some of the failures seemed fairly minor, at other times God's grace brought a hero from complete devastation into a new beginning of victory and success.

+ *Abraham* made a terrible mistake when he went along with his wife's idea to have a child by her servant, Hagar. Nevertheless, God later fulfilled His promise to give Abraham and Sarah their own offspring, and Isaac was born.

+ *Moses* had to overcome his failed attempt to deliver the Israelites from Egypt when he was age forty. At age eighty he was given a renewed call at the burning bush, and the Israelites were ultimately delivered.

+ *Samuel* apparently did a terrible job of raising his children. Still, God used him mightily. (See 1 Samuel 8:1–5.)

+ *David* had to recover from horrendous personal failures: adultery, deception, and murder. Nevertheless, because he repented and diligently sought the Lord, he has always been remembered not as a failure but as a man after God's heart. (See Acts 13:32.)

+ *John Mark* deserted the apostolic team of Barnabas and Paul, but later rebounded to write the gospel of Mark. (See Acts 15:38.)

The Flaw of Self-Reliance

One of my favorite examples of all is the apostle Peter, who experienced *extreme failure* before God brought him to a place of *extreme fruitfulness*. One of the remarkable things about Peter's story is that Jesus clearly knew all about Peter's weaknesses—yet He chose him anyway. Let me encourage you today: God knows all about *your* weaknesses and failures too, but His grace is able to restore you and give you the new beginning you need.

Peter was just a fisherman by trade. He wasn't the kind of guy you'd think of when looking for someone to be the spiritual leader of thousands of people. Yet Jesus didn't see Peter as we might have seen him: a crude, smelly, uneducated fishermen. Somehow, Jesus saw Peter as a person of great promise and destiny.

Peter had a fundamental weakness, but it wasn't what we might have assumed. We might have questioned Jesus' judgment, all right, but for completely different reasons. We may have asked, "Jesus, why would You pick someone who is so 'earthy'...so poor...so uneducated...so prone to arguments...so spiritually untrained?" But Jesus knew that Peter's real obstacle was something completely different than any of these outward factors: *He was full of pride and self-reliance.*

This character flaw is no minor issue! It goes to the very heart of whether or not we are truly usable by God. King Solomon—who seems to have had his own struggles with pride and self-reliance— warns us, *"Trust in the LORD with all your heart, and lean not on your own understanding"* (Proverbs 3:5). This is a difficult lesson for any of us to learn, and it was particularly hard for self-reliant Peter.

But God has His ways of helping us learn the lesson.

Peter always stood out among the other disciples, but not always for the best of reasons. Sometimes he stood out because he was the "star pupil"—the one who had the right answer to Jesus' probing questions. However, at other times he stood out because he easily became a dunce—someone prone to stick his foot in his mouth.

And in Peter's case, it was usually a quick turn-around from being a hero to being a dunce. Matthew 16:13–19 gives the wonderful account of Peter's revelation of Jesus' true identity. When the disciples were asked by Jesus, *"Who do you say that I am?"* (verse 15). Peter was ready with a quick, and correct, answer: *"You are the Christ, the Son of the living God"* (verse 16).

Good answer, Peter! Go to the head of the class! Jesus was so excited that He told Peter the entire church would be built upon this great revelation. Those who recognize Jesus as their Lord and Savior will be given *"the keys of the kingdom of heaven"* (verse 19).

Peter was undoubtedly feeling pretty impressed with himself at this point. But the chapter doesn't end there. Peter, who had just been applauded by Jesus, was about to say something stupid and get a major rebuke. The star pupil was about to get a needed taste of humility.

In Matthew 16:21–24, Jesus starts preparing His disciples for the cross. He tells them that they soon would be heading to Jerusalem, where He would suffer, be killed, and then be raised from the dead. From our vantage point a few thousand years later, this sounds like a pretty basic gospel message, but it horrified Peter: *"Then Peter took Him aside and began to rebuke Him, saying, 'Far be it from You, Lord; this shall not happen to You!'"* (verse 22).

Let's give Peter some credit here. He meant well. He was just trying to be loyal; trying to protect Jesus (and himself!) from harm; and trying to be the star pupil again by saying what he thought Jesus would want to hear. Have you ever had a great failure in your life when you were sincerely trying to do what you thought was best?

Peter must have been shocked by Jesus' response: *"Get behind Me, Satan! You are an offense to Me, for you are not mindful of the things of God, but the things of men"* (verse 23). Because of his pride and self-reliance, Jesus' star pupil had unwittingly put himself in league with Satan! It seems to have taken Peter mere moments to go from the mountaintop to the valley. Have you ever had a failure like that—right after feeling like you were on the top of the world?

It's too bad Peter couldn't have fully learned his lesson here, getting it over with once and for all. Yet rarely do we learn our lessons so quickly. If we look back over our lives, we'll see that we usually need several tries before we finally "get it right." In Peter's case, the episodes in Matthew 16 were just a "warm-up" for the trials still ahead.

The Greatest Trial

What is the biggest trial a person can face? This trial may come in many shapes and sizes, and may affect us in a variety of areas of our life. Yet it can be summarized in just two words: *the cross*! When Peter tried to challenge Jesus in Matthew 16, the issue was the cross. In fact, Jesus told Peter and the other disciples in that passage: *"If anyone desires to come after Me, let him deny himself, and take up his cross, and follow Me"* (Matthew 16:24).

When Jesus spoke of suffering and the cross, Peter was full of boasts and braggadocio: *"Lord, I am ready to go with You, both to prison and to death!"* (Luke 22:33). The cross? *No problem*, Peter thought.

But Jesus wasn't swayed by Peter's claims of loyalty and faithfulness. Despite Peter's boasts, Jesus knew that Peter would grievously deny Him. *"I tell you, Peter, the rooster shall not crow this day before you will deny three times that you know Me"* (Luke 22:34).

My friend, Jesus knows all about every sin you've ever committed or ever will commit. Yet the good news is that He loves you anyway. Not only that, but He also can see past your failure to a day of forgiveness, restoration, and new fruitfulness.

In Peter's case, Jesus not only predicted his failure, but He *also* predicted his restoration: *"Indeed, Satan has asked for you, that he may sift you as wheat. But I have prayed for you, that your faith should not fail; and when you have returned to Me, strengthen your brethren"* (Luke 22:31–32).

Isn't this a wonderful story? Even if you are about to fall into a terrible blunder, Jesus can see past your failures to a day when you will be restored and recommissioned for fruitful service. He knows you will experience failure at times but, as in the case of Peter, He is predicting your ultimate victory. He wants you to know that your failures can be overcome...and a new beginning is possible!

Although the Bible makes it clear that God can forgive us and restore us after we've fallen in some way, sometimes we struggle to forgive *ourselves*. Do you see how silly that is? The holy God who created the universe declares us *not guilty* because of the blood of His Son, but we feel as if we're still under God's condemnation.

Peter seems to have felt this same way. After he denied the Lord, he was heartbroken by what he had done. His old self-reliance was gone, but now the pendulum had swung completely to the other extreme: He didn't think Jesus could ever forgive him and use him again.

In John 21, we read that Peter returned to his previous life as a fisherman. Reading between the lines, it seems he figured his days in ministry were over. Instead of moving *forward* in the purposes of God, he determined that the best thing to do was to go *back*.

Yet Jesus had called Peter to a higher calling than his old life as a fisherman. He was called to be one of the *"fishers of men"* (Matthew 4:19). In a gentle and loving way, Jesus appears to Peter in John 21 and gives him another "miracle catch" of fish (as had happened earlier in Luke 5:1–11). Not only that, but Jesus also proceeded to recommission him for ministry: *"Feed My sheep"* (John 21:17).

Failure Doesn't Have to Be Final

If you have fallen in some way, my friend, can you hear Jesus' voice of forgiveness today? Can you see His desire to give you a new beginning and bless you again with abundance? Do you hear His heartbeat to restore you to fruitful service in His kingdom?

The ironic thing about Peter's failure is that it actually was a necessary part of his future success. Why? Because the old, arrogant, self-reliant Peter wasn't really usable by God! It wasn't until Peter was broken that he could truly understand his need for full reliance on God's grace and power.

The good news is that Jesus didn't allow Peter to wallow forever in a place of defeat and failure. Out of Peter's failure came forgiveness and restoration. He discovered God's grace in a new way, and on the day of Pentecost he became the "fisher of men" that Jesus had called him to be—and three thousand people were saved as a result. (See Acts 2.)

Perhaps you are struggling today with a stranglehold of failure in some area of your life. If so, the story of Peter can be a powerful message to you. By God's amazing grace, a fresh start is possible! Your failures don't have to be final!

TWENTY-EIGHT

WHEN YOU NEED TO GET UNSTUCK

I'm sure there are some people reading this book who feel it's simply too late for them to significantly change their lives or escape their negative circumstances. I can hear them now, wanting to tell me, "Bishop Bloomer, I wish I had read this book twenty or thirty years ago. Maybe I could have avoided making so many mistakes in my life. But now I'm pretty much stuck."

If this is how you're feeling, you're surely not alone. I've met countless people who feel like they're stuck at some crossroads in their life. Perhaps they are unemployed or in need of a new career. Or maybe they're feeling paralyzed by a health challenge or trapped in a toxic relationship. Many people, even in our churches, are stuck in some kind of addiction, unable to break free from drugs, alcohol, gambling, sexual perversion, or pornography. And lots of "good religious folks" seem stuck in an endless cycle of negative emotions, such as fear, anger, loneliness, or depression.

No matter what the cause may be, it's no fun to be stuck. Yet we've all felt that way at times. Fortunately, the Lord understands this plight, and He has a plan to help us break loose.

Getting a Hand Up

Acts 3:1–12 tells the story of a lame man who used to sit and beg outside the temple gate. He had been lame from birth, so he didn't really expect anything to change in his dismal circumstances.

Many Christians face a similar predicament today. Instead of truly entering into God's destiny for their lives, they are languishing outside the gate. And sadly, they're still looking to other people as their source rather than trusting God as the One who will intervene in their situation and meet their need.

But the story of the lame man has a happy ending, and this can be true in your life as well. One of my takeaways from this account is this:

> God wants you to encounter His love,
> so He can transform you by His power!

When the lame man woke up that day, all he could hope for was a handout. Doesn't that sound like a depressing way to live? Yet instead of a handout, God's plan was to give him a hand *up*.

This crippled man must have been shocked when Peter told him, *"In the name of Jesus Christ of Nazareth, **rise up and walk"** (verse 6).* He was being told to do the very thing that was impossible for him!

Friend, maybe God is speaking a similar message to *you* today. Perhaps He is telling you to forgive someone who seems impossible for you to forgive. Or He's telling you to break free from some addiction or unhealthy relationship you've been unsuccessful in breaking in the past. Remember: This is a new day. Quit looking back at your *past* when God speaks to you about your *future*!

This man by the temple gate had been stuck in his predicament for many years, but his life was about to change in a mere moment. Peter then *"took him by the right hand and **lifted him up**, and **immediately** his feet and ankle bones received strength"* (verse 7).

Do you see how this can give you hope for breaking free today? No matter how long you've been paralyzed in some area of your life—such as your health, finances, emotions, or relationships—God wants to lift you up.

Though you may have grown used to a life of sadness and regret, all that can change in a moment of time. Notice that it didn't take years of therapy for the lame man to recover: God changed his life *"immediately"*!

Also notice that the Lord wants to transform you from seeing yourself as a beggar, to realizing your birthright as His precious child. When that happens, you'll go from sitting aimlessly to *"walking, leaping, and praising God"* (verse 8). And instead of remaining *outside* the gates of God's purposes, you'll finally *enter in*: "[He] *stood and walked and entered the temple with them."*

The story ends by describing how those who witnessed the healing of the lame man were *"filled with wonder and amazement"* (verse 10). What a great lesson for you and me: People around us will be impacted for Christ whenever they see us get unstuck from some difficult situation in our life. They'll be filled with hope that what God has done for us, He can do for them as well.

TWENTY-NINE

STEPS TO YOUR BREAKOUT MOMENT

The longer I live, the more convinced I am that most people are paralyzed or imprisoned in some way. No wonder the Bible tells so many stories about those who got healed of paralysis or set free from bondage and imprisonment.

Yet, when we read such Bible stories today, it's easy to miss how these events apply to our lives. If we've never been physically paralyzed or lame, we can struggle to relate to the paralyzed man in Mark 2:1–12 or the lame man in Acts 3:1–12. And if we've never done jail time, we can assume there's not much we can learn from Joseph's release from an Egyptian dungeon (see Genesis 39–41) or the supernatural prison breaks of Peter (see Acts 12:1–19) and Paul and Silas (see Acts 16:16–40).

But, you see, the imprisonment most people face today is emotional and spiritual rather than physical. They've been traumatized by their journey through life, whether through the consequences of their own bad decisions or through the unkind actions of others.

In John 20:19–29, Jesus' disciples were locked in a self-imposed prison after experiencing the trauma of their Master's unjust arrest, brutal beating, and horrific crucifixion. Today we sometimes call those events "Good Friday," but there seemed nothing "good" about the cross of Calvary at the time. The disciples were understandably devastated, gathered together behind locked doors because of fear of the Jewish leaders.

Suddenly Jesus appeared to these shell-shocked men. Although preachers sometimes say, based on Revelation 3:20, that Jesus always *knocks* before entering our situation, that's simply not true. This time He just *came right on in*, bypassing every defense mechanism in order to release these traumatized followers from their emotional bondage.

This is one of the most pivotal scenes in the entire Bible. It's not an overstatement to say that the whole fate of the church and the expansion of God's kingdom rested on what would happen in the lives of these shattered men.

The disciples had left everything to follow Jesus, believing that their lives would ultimately change the world. Now their dreams seemed to have reached a cruel dead end. Dazed and confused, they were very unlikely candidates for any kind of heroic, world-changing mission.

Four Snares

So how did Jesus turn the *worst* of times into the *best* of times for these emotionally damaged followers? He addressed four different snares that were holding these men in spiritual captivity:

1. Fear

Not just once, but twice, Jesus told them, *"Peace be with you"* (John 20:19). And when they *"saw the Lord,"* their fear and anguish were replaced with great *joy* (verse 20). If you are feeling "stuck" in some area of your life today, it's likely that fear is one of the things holding you back. Just as He did for the disciples, Jesus wants to penetrate your closed doors and replace your fear with faith, and your anxiety with His peace and joy.

2. Purposelessness

These men who had taken such bold steps to leave their careers and families in order to change the world with Jesus were now left without a purpose or a vision. They had abandoned and denied their Savior in His hour of need, and now their traumatized condition seemed to disqualify them from any significant usefulness in His plan. Nevertheless, Jesus recommissioned and affirmed them with fresh vision and purpose: *"As the Father has sent Me, I also send you"* (verse 21). What an encouraging story for us today. Even when we feel like failures, unusable by God, He can reaffirm our calling and give us a new commission to impact the world.

3. Weakness

In addition to a lack of *purpose*, Jesus' disciples were suffering from a lack of *power*. A new commission would have fallen on deaf ears unless they also received new empowerment. Recognizing their need, Jesus breathed on them and said, *"Receive the Holy Spirit"* (verse 22). In their own strength, they never would have been able to fulfill His majestic plan for their lives—nor can you or I. But, empowered by the Spirit, we can transform the world. (See Acts 1:8; Philippians 4:13.)

4. Unforgiveness

Jesus showed them His wounds, proof that they had been forgiven by His shed blood. But then He talked to them about their calling to extend His forgiveness to others. If you are in some kind of spiritual prison today, there's a good chance that *forgiveness* is one of the keys needed to set you free. Perhaps you need to receive God's full forgiveness of your past, releasing you from any guilt, shame, or condemnation. Or maybe you are still locked in emotional bondage because you've not yet forgiven someone who has hurt you. Either way, forgiveness is an indispensable key to your spiritual and emotional freedom.

I encourage you to read through these four snares again, asking God to show you which of these four keys are needed to help you get unstuck and ready to fulfill your destiny as a follower of Christ.

Perhaps you've been hiding out behind closed doors for a long time now, traumatized by some experience that has been hard to shake. But if Jesus could take these distraught men from the shadow of the cross to the glory of resurrection life, surely He can transform *your* life and give you a new beginning.

Like Jesus' disciples, you may seem like an unlikely world-changer today. But once He has freed you from fear, given you fresh vision, empowered you by His Spirit, and dealt with your forgiveness issues, your life can be amazing. You don't have to wait any longer!

THIRTY

A QUICK FIX FOR YOUR "ISSUES"

The story is told in Mark 5:25–34 of a woman who suffered for twelve long years before coming to Jesus for a new beginning. Like so many of us today, she first tried *everything else* before seeking God for a remedy to her situation. She did the best she knew at the time, yet her efforts brought no relief. We are told that she *"had spent all that she had and was no better, but rather grew worse"* (Mark 5:26).

The King James translation describes this woman's trouble as *"an issue of blood"* (a bleeding problem). But before you write off her story as being irrelevant to you, consider this: we may not have *"an issue of blood,"* but each one of us faces some "issue" that we need God's help with.

Painful Issues

What is your "issue" today? Is it some kind of medical condition, like the woman in this story? Are you battling depression or some form of addiction? Do you face concerns about your finances or the choices being made by your children?

Perhaps your situation today feels much the same as for this distressed woman. You've tried just about everything, but nothing ever seems to change. What more can you do? Like this woman, your frustrating circumstances may have lingered for weeks, months, or even years. The devil tells you every day, "See, nothing will ever change! You might as well give up!"

The turning point in this woman's life began when some news gave her a glimpse of hope: *"After hearing about Jesus, she came up in the crowd behind Him and touched His cloak"* (Mark 5:27 NASB).

Although hearing about Jesus was the first step in the miracle this woman would receive, it was only the beginning. Lots of people hear about Jesus, but still don't get their breakthrough. Why not? Often they have failed to take the *next step* that this woman displayed.

After hearing about Jesus, she *took action* to touch His garments. There are many *hearers* in our churches today who have never become *doers*. (See James 1:22–25.) This woman received her healing because her *hearing* was followed by her *doing*.

What about you? You have heard about Jesus, and perhaps you even attend church regularly. But have you also taken the next step: pushing through the crowd to touch His garment? Sure, there probably are many obstacles. People may be in the way. Pain may be in the way. The devil himself may seem to block your path. However, you need to turn your desperation into obedient action, not letting anything stop you from getting to Jesus.

This woman's point of contact with Jesus was to touch His garment, but for us He may have some other action in mind. Perhaps He is calling us to a period of prayer and fasting. Are you ready to obey Him, whatever He tells you to do?

Speak in Faith

Notice that this woman did something amazing while she was still waiting for the breakthrough: She spoke words of faith: *"She said, 'If only I may touch His clothes, I shall be made well'"* (Mark 5:28).

Many believers are willing to give a testimony *after* their breakthrough comes, but during their time of testing they are full of moaning and groaning. But I love the fact that this woman proclaimed the victory before she received it! She not only *believed* in her heart, but she also *spoke* words of faith from her lips. Her example shows how powerful our words can be. As Solomon challenges us in Proverbs 18:21, *"Death and life are in the power of the tongue…."* This woman's *life* was literally spared by the faith she exercised and proclaimed.

If you need a new beginning today, what kind of words are you speaking? Many people speak words of hopelessness and defeat:

+ "Things will never change, I guess."

+ "These trials seem to be my cross to bear."

+ "Maybe God doesn't love me. Perhaps this is His judgment for my sins."

It's time to quit talking like this! We need to start speaking what God says about us in His Word:

+ "God is for me, and He will overcome anything that comes against me."

+ "Jesus came to give me life, and life more abundantly."

+ "Nothing can separate me from God's love."

+ "Because of God's love for me, I am able to overcome any attacks of the enemy."

My friend, don't *wait* for the victory before you start *proclaiming* it! Your testimony of faith is one of the greatest keys to becoming an overcomer. (See Revelation 12:10–11.) You need to get away from the naysayers and the purveyors of gloom and doom. Surround yourself with those who point you to Jesus and stand with you to believe that a breakthrough is on the way.

This woman discovered that Jesus was able to quickly fix her "issue," and the same is true for your today. A fresh start is available in Jesus. He wants to speak words of freedom, healing, and deliverance to you, just as He did to the afflicted woman: *"Daughter, your faith has made you well. Go in peace, and be healed of your affliction"* (Mark 5:34). Receive His promise to *you* today!

THIRTY-ONE

BREAK LOOSE FROM SICKNESS

We saw in the last chapter how the woman afflicted for twelve years was instantly healed when she touched the hem of Jesus' garment. I love that story, but I want to go a little deeper on the subject of how you can break loose from sickness.

With all my heart, I believe it's God's will for you and your loved ones to be healed today. If you need a healing in your body, your emotions, your finances, your family, or some other area of your life, God's Word is clear that He wants you to *"prosper in all things and be in health, just as your soul prospers"* (3 John 1:2).

The Lord is so desirous of our health that He even describes Himself as our Healer or Doctor if we obey His voice:

> *If you will listen carefully to the voice of the LORD your God and do what is right in his sight, obeying his commands and keeping all his decrees, then I will not make you suffer any of the diseases I sent on the Egyptians; for I am the LORD who heals you.*
> (Exodus 15:26 NLT)

So why are so many Christians in poor health today? There are many factors, of course, and someday I hope to write a book on God's principles for good health. Practically, many of us could use more exercise. And I've known many believers who are literally "killing themselves with their fork" (i.e., by what they eat).

But more basically, the Bible says the Lord's people often are *"destroyed for lack of knowledge"* (Hosea 4:6). Too often, we forfeit the blessings of health and prosperity because we don't know the necessary steps to receive them.

If you or a loved one is struggling with some kind of medical condition, here are six important steps to keep in mind as you're seeking a healing touch from God.

1. Eliminate Any Hindrances

Ask the Holy Spirit to convict you of such things as unbelief, unforgiveness, pride, occult involvement, sexual sins, generational sins, poor choices, and fear. If you realize you've displeased the Lord in some way, repent—and repent quickly. Then ask God to relieve you of anxiety and stress as you prepare the way for His healing power to flow in your spirit, soul, and body.

2. Worship

Remember how King Jehoshaphat's army was so outnumbered by the enemy that it didn't stand a chance? (See 2 Chronicles 20.) What did Jehoshaphat do? God told him to appoint singers to go out ahead of the army and *worship*.

The Bible records the miraculous result: "*When they began to sing and to praise, the* Lord *set ambushes against the* [enemies]...*and they were defeated*" (verse 22). What a lesson! If we choose to worship the Lord when faced with poor health or other challenging circumstances, God will give us victory! So remember to start giving the Lord honor and praise whenever you or a loved one is overwhelmed by a health crisis.

Worship is a great key for unleashing God's supernatural power in your life. It will also help you take your eyes off your circumstances and completely surrender yourself to Him. And it signals your recognition that He alone holds the answers to your health and that you can't resolve your problems in your own strength.

3. Pray the Word

Isaiah 55:11 reveals the amazing power of God's Word to transform our circumstances: "[My Word]...*shall* **not** *return to Me void, but it* **shall** *accomplish what I please, and it* **shall** *prosper in the thing* *for which I sent it."* When your prayers are based on His Word, God promises to accomplish what you are asking Him to do!

Ask the Holy Spirit to lead you to Scripture passages concerning your health. Psalm 107:20 says, *"He sent His word and healed them, and delivered them from their destructions."* And His Word is even compared to medicine:

> *My child, pay attention to what I say. Listen carefully to my words. Don't lose sight of them. Let them penetrate deep into your heart, for they bring life to those who find them, and healing to their whole body.* (Proverbs 4:20–22 NLT)

Let those words sink in for a moment. God says when we pay attention to His words and allow them to penetrate deeply into our heart, our *"whole body"* will be healed!

As you study God's promises for your healing, I encourage you to *personalize* the Bible promises on healing. Here's an example based on Isaiah 43:1–2:

> The Lord, my Creator, says that I am not to be afraid about my health, because He has redeemed me, spirit, soul, and body. He has called me by name, and I am His! When I pass through the waters and feel as though I'm drowning in my sickness, He has promised to be with me and save me. When it seems as though I'm walking through fires of disease, I will not be scorched. Because of His love and protection, the flames of adversity won't burn me. Amen!

And you can also personalize Isaiah 53:4–5 like this:

> Thank You, Lord Jesus, that You have borne by griefs and carried my sorrows. I'm so grateful that You willingly chose to be wounded for my transgressions and bruised for my iniquities. Thank You for paying the price on the cross for my sins, my peace, and my healing.

Meditate on and declare Scripture verses like these throughout the day to encourage and strengthen yourself when you're feeling sick and weary and are tempted to be hopeless about your health. Faith will rise, and God will use that faith to release His healing power in your body.

4. Wage Spiritual War

Too often, modern-day Christians forget that there is a spiritual component to health. It's not just a matter of bacteria, viruses, or tumors. Several verses point out that the devil often has a role in bringing illness to the people of God. (See Acts 10:38; Luke 13:16.)

This means you must be aware of Satan's strategies to rob you of your health (see John 10:10), and make sure you put on the whole armor of God to resist him (see Ephesians 6:14–17). You can overcome the enemy's attacks by the mighty spiritual weapons God has given you. (See 2 Corinthians 10:4.)

Through Christ, you have the power to defeat Satan's attacks against your health. When your life is submitted to God's authority, you can tell the devil, "Stay out of my life!"—and he must flee. (See James 4:7.)

5. Ask God for Wisdom

As you get advice and make decisions about your health, it's imperative that you follow Solomon's guidance and *"get wisdom"* (Proverbs 4:7). The world, your doctor, and well-meaning family and friends may all have opinions about what you should do when you need healing. But instead of blindly following every offer of health advice, you must ask God for His wisdom and let His peace steer your heart. (See Colossians 3:15.)

So *be wise!* Don't make a major health decision until you have peace in your heart. Sometimes you have to wait for His instructions and His healing touch. While He may give you an instantaneous miracle, at other times the healing will be more gradual. And I've even seen the Lord direct me to specific medical products and procedures that were very beneficial to my health.

Even as you are consulting with medical practitioners, don't lose sight of this vital truth: God *wants* to heal you! He's your *Jehovah-Rapha*—the God who heals *all* your diseases. (See Psalm 103:3.) And if you don't receive your healing right away, remember that the Lord's promises are fulfilled in our lives *"through faith and **patience"*** (Hebrews 6:12). So go ahead and praise Him while you *wait!*

6. Touch Him by Faith

After you've done everything else, I encourage you to go back to the example of the woman who had suffered with a hemorrhage for twelve years. (See Mark 5:25–34.) Press through the crowd and the obstacles, and touch Jesus by faith, asking Him for the healing you need.

My friend, you can be healed *today* in Jesus' mighty name!

THIRTY-TWO

BREAK LOOSE FROM DEPRESSION

Depression is a complicated subject, with many different definitions, approaches, connotations, and proposed remedies. I probably could write an entire book on what the Bible says about depression, and there's certainly not enough space here to share everything that needs to be said on the subject. But I want to briefly touch on it because it specifically has thrown so many of God's people into bondage.

In fact, many of the Bible's greatest heroes encountered times of depression. Even Jesus Himself said shortly before going to the cross, *"My soul is exceedingly sorrowful, even to death"* (Matthew 26:38). And the apostle Paul spoke of a very gloomy time in his life: *"We were burdened beyond measure, above strength, so that we despaired even of life."* Paul eventually concluded that there was a *purpose* in the trials he encountered: *"...that we should not trust in ourselves but in God who raises the dead"* (2 Corinthians 1:8–9).

Sometimes people in the Scriptures expressed bewilderment about *why* they were experiencing depression. For example, *The Message* paraphrases Psalm 42: *"Why are you down in the dumps, dear soul? Why are you crying the blues?"* (verse 5). The psalmist is struggling to figure out why he's feeling down, when things were great just a short time before:

> I was always at the head of the worshiping crowd, right out in front,
> leading them all, eager to arrive and worship, shouting praises,
> singing thanksgiving—celebrating, all of us, God's feast!

> (verse 4 MSG)

Maybe you can relate to what the psalmist is describing here. I sure can. Sometimes I've been on the mountaintop after preaching a powerful word from God, and only minutes later I'm down in the valley.

The Cause of Depression

Depression can have a variety of causes. If we incorrectly diagnose the source of our depression, we'll be ineffective in eradicating it. Here are just a few of the causes of depression found in the Bible:

+ *Sin, disobedience, and rebellion*: We see this in the case of Cain, who was downcast after killing his brother Abel. (See Genesis 4:6–7.)

+ *Physical causes, such as hunger or fatigue*: This happened to Elijah after he defeated the false prophets of Baal and was threatened by Jezebel. (See 1 Kings 19:2–14.) His depression improved after he got some extra sleep, ate some food, and heard God's voice again.

+ *Demonic attacks*: Isaiah 61:3 says God wants to give us a *"garment of praise"* to replace a *"spirit of heaviness"* (NIV says *"spirit of despair"*). Satan has his demonic hordes working overtime to depress the people of God these days.

Whatever the cause of our depression may be, the Lord wants to bring us healing, refreshing, and joy. We need to surround ourselves with friends who can encourage in the Lord. (See 1 Samuel 23:16.) And we also must learn how to encourage *ourselves* in the Lord (see 1 Samuel 30:6), by coming into His presence and meditating on His Word.

Friend, I don't know what kinds of difficult, depressing situations you may be facing today. But I do know that God cares about you and can set you free from your depression when you cry out to Him.

The Solution to Depression

So what's the solution when we feel overwhelmed by depression? The psalmist gives us some tips:

When my soul is in the dumps, I rehearse everything I know
of you.... Then GOD *promises to love me all day, sing songs all*
through the night! My life is God's prayer.... Fix my eyes on
God—soon I'll be praising again. He puts a smile on my face.
He's my God.   (Psalm 42:6–8, 11 MSG)

It's not always easy to break loose from depression, but the
psalmist is on the right track here. Instead of focusing on his melan-
choly state of mind, he turns his attention to the Lord and begins to
rehearse his blessings.

He also makes a very important observation: his depression
won't last forever, because God would soon put a smile on his face
again. Nothing ousts depression faster than *hope*. When we recognize that a better day is ahead, depression loses its power over us.

Like the psalmist, Paul understood the need to focus on our
blessings instead of on our negative circumstances:

Brethren, whatever things are true, whatever things are noble,
whatever things are just, whatever things are pure, whatever
things are lovely, whatever things are of good report, if there is
any virtue and if there is anything praiseworthy—meditate on
these things.... And the God of peace will be with you.
                                    (Philippians 4:8–9)

What an important reminder for all of us. Yes, we may face
depressing circumstances at times. Paul was in *prison* when he wrote
these words! But regardless of what may be happening around us, *"the*
God of peace" will be with us when our eyes are on Him and we put
our attention on His blessings in our life.

One day King David found himself surrounded by problems:

LORD, *how they have increased who trouble me! Many are*
they who rise up against me.
Many are they who say of me, "There is no help for him in
God."   (Psalm 3:1–2)

Perhaps you're facing a similar experience, questioning whether God will come to your aid. David's conclusion should be an encouragement for you to keep trusting God, even when You don't see His answers right away: *"But You, O Lord, are a shield for me, my glory and the One who lifts up my head"* (verse 3).

When the difficult circumstances of life weigh you down, God offers to come and lift up your head. In Jesus' mighty name, your depression will have to leave!

THIRTY-THREE

BREAK LOOSE FROM FEAR

Some of the most beautiful words in all of Scripture, in my opinion, are found in Matthew 25:21: *"Well done, good and faithful servant; you were faithful over a few things, I will make you ruler over many things. Enter into the joy of your lord."*

Each one of us should long to hear these breathtaking words when we stand before the Lord in eternity one day. But in order to receive this greeting, we will have to be set free from fear. Of all the strongholds that keep people from fulfilling their calling and destiny, fear is probably the most common.

Make no mistake about it: Fear is your enemy, not your friend. The Bible is quite clear about this: *"God has not given us a spirit of fear, but of power and of love and of a sound mind"* (2 Timothy 1:7). Over and over again in the pages of His Word, God tells people: "Fear not!"

Before we go any further, I want you to pause and ask yourself what you would do if you had no fear of failure, no fear of harm, no fear of financial lack, no fear of rejection. What mighty work would you endeavor for God's kingdom if you knew beyond a shadow of a doubt that you had His favor, provision, and protection?

Parable of the Talents

Jesus' statement about the *"good and faithful servant"* comes in the context of the parable of the talents in Matthew 25:14–30. Before going on a long journey, the master had entrusted his possessions to three different servants. The first servant was given five talents (a currency of silver) and the second servant was given two talents.

The master was pleased with *both* of the first two servants. Although they had been given different amounts, they each had invested wisely, doubling the amount they initially received. The first two servants each received exactly the same words of praise from their master. Pleased with their faithful stewardship, he gave them his favor and said, "*Well done.*"

The first two servants both had taken steps of faith to invest their master's resources, and they each received an *increase* as a result. Because they had been "*faithful over a few things,*" the master made them "*ruler over **many** things*" (see verses 21, 23).

What a fantastic picture of the scene in heaven for those who are faithful with the resources God entrusted to them on earth. Can you imagine what it will be like to hear your Master embrace you and say...

"Enter into the joy of your Lord!"

Too often, I meet believers who complain that they haven't been given much to invest into God's kingdom and the work of spreading the gospel. "I hardly have enough to provide for my own family," they say.

Yet the master in the parable of the talents didn't judge his servants on the basis of how many resources they started with—he judged them on their faithfulness to *invest* and *increase* whatever resources they had been given. By doubling their investment, the first two servants received a *100 percent return!*

But there was another servant in this story—one who missed out on his master's favor. Instead of investing the money he had been given, he chose to bury it. Apparently he assumed the master would be pleased just to get his money back when he returned.

But instead of being pleased, the master was livid, calling the man a "*wicked and lazy servant*" (Matthew 25:26). While the third servant thought he was playing it safe by burying his money in the ground, his cowardice ended up costing him everything. The master gave his money to another, the servant who had grown his investment from five to ten talents.

This outcome may seem harsh to us, but we need to see what had motivated the man to make such a tragic error:

> *"Lord, I knew you to be a hard man, reaping where you have not sown, and gathering where you have not scattered seed. And I was **afraid**, and went and **hid your talent** in the ground. Look, there you have what is yours."* (verses 24–25)

You see, it was *fear* that had hindered this man from investing his master's resources. Unwilling to take a risk, he hid the resources where he thought they would remain safe.

Look how this servant allowed *fear* to sabotage *God's favor* in his life:

+ *Fear* prevented him from acting in *faith*.

+ By failing to act in *faith*, he was unable to be *faithful* with the master's resources.

+ Because he wasn't *faithful*, he forfeited the *favor* and *increase* he would have received from the master.

How blind this servant was! Everyone else in this parable took steps of faith instead of steps of fear. The master and the first two servants were sowers, investing the resources they had and expecting an increase. *The only one who failed to receive an increase was the third servant—because fear kept him from investing!*

My friend, which of the servants are you most like today? If you allow fear to govern your life, you will miss out on the amazing favor and abundance God wants to give you as His son or daughter. So never let fear hold you back from taking bold steps of faith to serve the Lord and advance His kingdom.

I'm asking the Lord to deliver you from any fears today. When you're delivered from fear, you will courageously invest your life and your resources into God's kingdom and the lives of others, confident that you'll receive His bountiful provision and favor. Best of all, instead of fear and frustration, you'll be able to *"enter into the joy of your lord."*

THIRTY-FOUR

BREAK LOOSE FROM POVERTY

People are often shocked when I suggest that the world's economic challenges during the past decade may actually be a blessing in disguise. Why? Because these difficult times are compelling many Christians to reassess whether they're truly trusting in the Lord as their source of every good thing.

It's one thing to claim we're trusting in God for our provision when we have a good job, great home value, and a growing 401(k) fund for our retirement. But what happens to our faith when the whole financial system is shaking and our resources seem to be drying up instead of growing? What if we're struggling just to pay our bills and keep our car from being repossessed?

Friend, it has never been more important for God's people to learn the secrets of coming to Him as *Jehovah-Jireh*—our faithful Provider—even when every human resource seems to be failing us. Instead of trying to find hope in our circumstances, the Lord wants us to look to *Him* for overflowing abundance that has nothing to do with the economic systems of this world!

Part of the problem is that many Christians have forgotten where their true citizenship is. What about you? If I asked you which country you're a citizen of, how would you respond? Perhaps you would say, "I'm a citizen of the United States" or "I live in Canada or the United Kingdom." If I pressed a little further and asked how things were *going* in your country, you might say, "The economy is pretty sluggish right now, which is making life pretty hard for me."

However, consider this: The Bible says *our citizenship is in heaven"* (Philippians 3:20). Heaven is a "country" where there's never been a recession or economic downturn. In heaven there's no poverty or lack, nor is there any sickness or broken relationship. God's heavenly kingdom is like no country we've ever seen on earth, and there's never been a foreclosure or bankruptcy there!

But most of us Christians in Western nations today are much too earthbound—wrapped up in this world instead of looking to God's kingdom as our source of provision. We've forgotten the Bible's clear instruction: *"Set your mind on things above, not on things on the earth"* (Colossians 3:2). As a result, we've put our hope in man's economy instead of God's.

To put things in perspective, it's helpful to look at the journey of the Israelites from Egypt to the Promised Land. This word picture describes three distinct "lands" people can live in regarding God's abundance. Whether you know it or not, *you* are living in one of these three lands today:

+ Egypt: The Land of "Not Enough"

  When the children of Israel lived in Egypt, they were slaves to cruel taskmasters and given only meager rations of food. (See Exodus 1.)

+ The Wilderness: The Land of "Barely Enough"

  After being delivered from their bondage and scarce provisions in Egypt, the Israelites wandered for forty years in the wilderness. Despite their failure to consistently trust and obey the Lord, He met all their needs in the wilderness—but just barely. He provided manna for them to eat each day, but it couldn't be stored up, nor were there any leftovers. (See Exodus 16:14–21.) During this stage of their journey, God's people were *surviving*, but not *thriving*.

+ Canaan: The Land of "More than Enough"

  The Israelites probably got used to their daily routine of gathering manna and having barely enough. But God had so much *more* planned for them in the Promised Land (Canaan). Scripture describes it as *"exceedingly good"* with huge crops, and a land that *"flows with milk and honey"* (Numbers 14:7–8).

Which of these three lands are *you* living in today? Sadly, most Christians seem to be living in the land of "Not Enough" or "Barely Enough." Their joy in life goes up and down with the daily stock market reports, or they're anxious every month about whether they'll even be able to make their rent or car payment.

But this is not how God wants us to live! You don't have to die and go to heaven to begin experiencing the "Land of More than Enough"!

When the Israelites left the wilderness and passed over the Jordan River into the Promised Land, they were entering a whole new economy.

Soon God's daily supply of manna stopped, and He began supplying their needs in a very different way. Instead of living hand-to-mouth on their daily ration of manna from heaven, the Lord's people were entering into a land of abundance, where they could *"eat food without scarcity"* and *"not lack anything"* (Deuteronomy 8:9 NASB).

My friend, I'm convinced that God wants to bring you into a new dimension of blessing and prosperity today. He wants to break off your chains of poverty and lack. Instead of the bondage of Egypt or the scarcity of the wilderness, He wants to bring you into a whole new economy—the *Land of More than Enough*!

THIRTY-FIVE

YOU CAN BE AN OVERCOMER

Throughout history, the greatest heroes have been those who've had the greatest challenges to overcome. But isn't it curious that while everyone wants to be an overcomer, we're typically upset when we're actually given something to *overcome*?

That's exactly what happened to Jesus' disciples when suddenly confronted with *"a furious squall"* (verse 37 NIV), on the Sea of Galilee one day (Mark 4:37 NIV).

Perhaps you're facing a storm of a different kind today. Not *"a furious squall"* but rather a furious boss, spouse, child, or creditor. Or maybe you're struggling against stormy winds in your health or emotions.

The tempest on the Sea of Galilee that day was so fierce that the boat was *"nearly swamped,"* and the terrified disciples thought they were going to drown. Life's storms are a lot like *terrorists*—popping up when we least expect and doing everything they can to engender *fear* in our heart.

However, this brief story contains six powerful lessons for how we can not only survive the storms of life, but be even *better off* because of them:

1. Remember the promise.

The story begins with Jesus saying, *"Let us go over to the other side"* (verse 35 NIV). If the disciples had been paying attention, they would have noticed Jesus' resolve to bring them *over*, not letting them go *under*! And I'm convinced He has the same plan for *you* today. He didn't say you would drown on the way to your destination, He said you would arrive there. So no matter how scary the storm may seem, you can be confident He will bring you safely to *"the other side."*

2. Leave the crowd behind.

If you're truly an overcomer, it's unlikely you'll also be Mr. or Ms. Popularity. In fact, verse 36 describes the disciples *"leaving the crowd behind."* Why is that significant? Because a lot of people in *"the crowd"* aren't on track to be overcomers. They're content to live mediocre, uneventful lives. Rather than risk facing any storms on their journey to the other side of the lake, they would prefer to camp out safely in the harbor. But remember: You'll never make a significant impact if you refuse to take risks or venture out into the deeper waters.

3. Make sure you're taking Jesus with you—on the inside.

This is so basic, but so easy to overlook. One day even His father and mother forgot to bring Jesus along with them. (See Luke 2:41–50.) But here we're told the disciples *"took him along"* (verse 36 NIV). If you're going through a storm, it sure is good to have Jesus in the boat with you. It's fascinating that *"there were also other boats with him"* (verse 36 NIV). Jesus was only in the one boat, but other boats were following along nearby. This is an apt depiction of people who attend church or other religious events in order to get in the *vicinity* of Christ, yet they've never really invited Him into *their own* boat. Until a storm hits, they probably feel safe enough with the status quo, but the storm reveals how dangerous it is to *assume* Jesus is in your boat, when He truly isn't. When you're going through rough waters, you don't just want the Savior outside your boat—you desperately need Him on the *inside*.

4. Don't doubt His love for you.

Seeing Jesus asleep amid the storm, the disciples reacted the same way we would. Waking Him up, they questioned His love for them: *"Teacher, don't you care if we drown?"* (verse 38 NIV).

Their logic was flawed, but we've all wondered the same thing at times: "Lord, if You *really* loved us, You wouldn't allow us to go through storms like this!" But as the old children's song says, "Jesus loves me, this I know, for the Bible tells me so." Instead of doubting His love while we're experiencing a storm, we should allow Him to show Himself strong and faithful in the storm.

5. Be patient when you're halfway across.

When Jesus told you He would get you to the other side of the lake, He meant it. But being in transition is difficult, and sometimes the journey lasts a lot longer than we would like. At times it can even be tempting to go *back* to the shore we came from instead of *forward* to the other side. Yet we must not lose heart when we're halfway there!

6. Stir up your faith.

After Jesus calmed the storm, He asked His disciples, "*Why are you so afraid? Do you still have no faith?*" (verse 40 NIV). Although the disciples had to awaken *Jesus* in this story, that's not really the message for us, for Jesus isn't asleep today. Instead, it's *our faith* in Him that must be awakened.

The prophet Isaiah cried out to God in despair: "*There is no one who calls on Your name, who stirs himself up to take hold of You*" (Isaiah 64:7). Isaiah's observation holds a vital key for whatever breakthrough you may be seeking in your life today: You must "stir yourself" to take hold of the Lord!

You see, storms can be our friend rather than our enemy, because they're meant to cause us to awaken our faith. Rather than being a one-time proposition, this is something we must do on a regular basis. Paul told Timothy to "*kindle afresh the gift of God which is in you*" (2 Timothy 1:6 NASB). Other translations say we must "*stir up*" (NKJV) or "*fan into flame*" (NIV) the gifts and callings of God in our lives.

My friend, God is calling you to be an overcomer, not a casualty or a victim. When you trust the Lord and apply these six lessons, life's storms will always lift you higher.

THIRTY-SIX

GOD'S PLAN TO REDEEM SEX

I don't know whether to be amused or annoyed when I hear people imply that God is opposed to sex. How could He be opposed to it, when He's the one who *created* it?

However, sex is a very powerful force, and the Bible gives us clear instructions for how it is to be used. When used in the proper way, it's a lot like a nuclear power plant—creating energy to make the world a better place. But when we violate God's instructions, sex becomes more like a nuclear *bomb*—causing incredible havoc and destruction.

Think about it: The power of nuclear energy is able to light a city or destroy the city. It's all in how the energy is used.

Sex is no different. God established it to be a great blessing to humankind and the means by which we propagate the human race. But throughout history, unbridled sex has also unleashed countless divorces, given birth to fatherless children, destroyed reputations, and even led to murders. Numerous politicians have been brought down because of their sexual appetites, and sometimes entire nations have been affected.

As a preacher, I'm saddened to see the destructive impact that misplaced sex often has on people's lives. From child molestation to out-of-wedlock births and adultery, the "nuclear energy" of sex often brings damage instead of blessing.

Think of it this way…

Every car comes with an owner's manual—the manufacturer's instruction guide for how the vehicle should be maintained and utilized. God, the creator of sex, knows best how to use it, don't you think? The Bible is our "manufacturer's handbook," and we ignore its instructions at our own peril.

Even though the Bible testifies that God blesses sex in its rightful context, it troubles me that many in our society have built their entire lives around unbridled sexual experiences. In the process, they've made a personal altar to the god of Pleasure.

You see, sex can easily become an idol—and God definitely doesn't like idols.

In today's culture, many people place only minimal and extremely subjective restrictions on permissible sexual activity. For example, they don't confine sexual relations to marriage, but instead argue you should only sleep with people you truly have "feelings" for. And, of course, don't forget to use a condom, so the sex will be "safe." Other than these few warnings, they say "anything goes" if it's between "consenting adults."

Just because sex is a God-inspired force, that certainly doesn't mean it is permissible or wise in every situation. The mantra "if it feels good, do it" is more appropriate for dogs than for well-adjusted, mature people.

But the problem isn't just the misuse of sex by those who insist on violating God's "owner's manual." I'm also grieved by the failure of many godly, monogamous couples to devote enough time and energy to this vital area of intimacy and enjoyment. Instead of preachers only railing against sexual excesses, we should also be *promoting sexual freedom* in the bedrooms of every husband and wife.

If you still believe God is a killjoy, I have something for you to read. It's called the Song of Solomon, and it's one of the books in the Bible. Yes, God devoted an entire book to advocating sex and romantic love. Even if this has been a painful area of your life, it's never too late for redemption.

But if sex has become a stumbling block and idol in your life, it may be time to devote yourself to a season of prayer and a study of the Scriptures on sexual purity. You must not continue allowing the devil to pervert something God originally designed as pure and holy.

I meet many people who still think of sex as dirty, sinful, shameful, evil, and even embarrassing. Well, I'm sure it *can* be any of those things, but that's certainly not how God created it.

Perhaps you wonder how I can be so certain of this. Maybe you want to ask at this point, "George, a lot of damage has been done in my life because of sex. How can you be so sure God created it to be holy and wholesome, instead of evil and destructive?"

The answer is found in Genesis 1:31, a powerful statement about God's original creation: "*God saw everything that He had made, and indeed it was very good.*" This is a beautiful verse, isn't it? God said that *everything* He made was good. Not just some things, but *all* things.

Sex is part of the "*everything*" God made. He didn't say He made it dirty or shameful. He said He made it good. In fact, He made it *very good!*

So when it comes to sex, God wants you to "get it right." This means following His instructions. Hebrews 13:4 says, "*Marriage should be honored by all, and the marriage bed kept pure*" (NIV).

I like how *The Message* paraphrases this verse: "*Honor marriage, and guard the sacredness of sexual intimacy between wife and husband. God draws a firm line against casual and illicit sex.*" Do you see why God "*draws a firm line*" against infidelity? So that you can "*guard the sacredness of sexual intimacy.*"

Perhaps you've never considered sex to be something "sacred" and holy, but that's exactly how God intends it to be. If your sexual life is still a long way from God's intended standard, don't despair. He still can transform you through the "renewing of your mind" on this important subject. (See Romans 12:2.)

God wants your sexual experiences to be *blessed*. He wants to give you His best. But this can only happen when you are willing to trust Him, obey His instructions, and wait for Him to fulfill His perfect plan for your life.

So remember: God's best is beyond your wildest dreams—and His best is worth waiting for!

THIRTY-SEVEN

THE BLESSINGS AND DANGERS OF "ONE FLESH"

Genesis 2:24–25 provides God's foundational statement about healthy, holy marital sex: *"A man shall leave his father and mother and be joined to his wife, and they shall become one flesh. And they were both naked, the man and his wife, and were not ashamed."*

The Lord created this to be a great blessing for humankind—not just to procreate, but as a source of pleasure and intimacy as well. The "one flesh" principle beautifully portrays the *delight* of sex within marriage and the *danger* of sex outside of marriage. It's not a step to take lightly!

The passage ends by saying that Adam and Eve were *naked* and *unashamed*. You see, guilt and shame were never meant to be a part of marital sex. Shame is something that never affected Adam and Eve until after they disobeyed God in Genesis 3. And sex had absolutely nothing to do with it.

Do you see how awesome it can be to have guilt-free sex? Naked, unashamed, and uninhibited. That's how God always intended it to be.

But if you truly grasp this principle, you'll see why there's really no such thing as "casual sex." The act of sexual intercourse inevitably bonds you to the other person—not just physically, but also emotionally and spiritually.

The apostle Paul used these verses in Genesis to warn the Corinthian Christians about the detrimental consequences of sex outside of marriage. Prostitution and other kinds of immorality were rampant in Corinth, and Paul wanted the believers there to understand the emotional and spiritual dangers of such activities: *"Do you not know that he who unites himself with a prostitute is one with her in body? For it is said, 'The two will become one flesh'"* (1 Corinthians 6:16 NIV).

Purity of Eyes, Head, and Heart

However, sexual purity means a lot more than just abstaining from the act of sex. The Bible makes it clear that purity is also a matter of the *eyes*, the *head*, and the *heart*.

You probably remember the story of Job, the man of God who was severely tormented by Satan for a period of time. His friends assumed his trials were the judgment of God for some kind of hidden sin in Job's life, but they were wrong.

Job spent a considerable amount of time defending himself to his friends, and sexual purity was one of the issues he covered. Not only had Job been faithful to his marriage vows, but he assured his friends that he had taken an additional step—making a commitment not to lust after other women. *"I made a covenant with my eyes,"* he told them (Job 31:1 NIV).

You see, sexual purity starts with a commitment to guard your *heart*, and that means being careful about what you *look at*. This is a tough assignment in today's sex-crazed culture. How can you guard your eyes when scantily clad women or men are on every billboard and magazine cover, not to mention the nudity that pervades modern movies and TV shows? And if you're a fan of rap music, you may need to make a covenant with your *ears* as well as your eyes.

Yet I run into many naive people who say it doesn't matter what you fantasize about, as long as you don't actually do the act. How foolish and delusional!

The old maxim is true:

Sow a thought...reap an action.
Sow an action...reap a habit.

Sow a habit…reap a lifestyle.
Sow a lifestyle…reap a destiny.

You see, it all begins with a thought. That's why the apostle Paul wrote that we must bring *"every thought into captivity to the obedience of Christ"* (2 Corinthians 10:5).

My friend, you will become what you *think* about, not just what you *do*. And you're just kidding yourself if you think you can build a fire of lust in your heart without the fire eventually spreading to your actions.

No wonder Solomon asked, *"Can a man take fire to his bosom, and his clothes not be burned?"* (Proverbs 6:27). In comparing sexual passion to fire, Solomon is making a profound point. Like sex, fire can be a powerful force for good. Yet fire can also be dangerous if it gets out of hand. When the fire is in a fireplace, it warms the house, bringing joy and comfort. But if fire breaks out of its proper boundaries, it can burn the house down!

The bottom line is this: *"Guard your heart above all else, for it determines the course of your life"* (Proverbs 4:23 NLT). As Job recognized, this process begins with guarding the gateways of your eyes and ears. This is no small issue, for *"it determines the course of your life."*

A Covenant with Your Eyes

There are three very practical things you can do in order to make *"a covenant with [your] eyes"* (Job 31:1). First, you need to be careful about the movies you watch, the music you listen to, the websites you visit, and the way you look at members of the opposite sex. I know this can be hard, but God wants to help you. He will give you the wisdom, discernment, and strength you need!

The second vital step is to make sure you have trusted Christian friends or a counselor to hold you accountable in guarding your heart and maintaining sexual purity. You don't have to walk alone in your quest for sexual purity.

Finally, if you are married, I encourage you not to neglect your sexual relationship. This is an important part of a healthy marriage, as Paul pointed out in 1 Corinthians 7:1–5. I realize that it often will require both sensitivity and courage to address these kinds of issues with your spouse. But if your sex life is sporadic or nonexistent, Satan will do his best to exploit the situation.

Remember: When you are seeking an enjoyable sex life in your marriage, *God is on your side!* He will help you break loose from anything hindering it from happening.

THIRTY-EIGHT

DISCOVER THE FAVOR FACTOR

When I preach on breaking loose from the things hindering us from God's best for our lives, sometimes people get the wrong idea. Often they've been bound up in some kind of negative habit or relationship for a long time, and it sounds like it will surely be *hard work* to break free.

Well, I'll be honest: God may require you to take some steps of faith and obedience in order to break loose. He may tell you it's time to be more disciplined about studying His Word, praying, or worshipping. Or He may instruct you to go into rehab, join an accountability group, find a good Christian counselor, or even have a demon cast out.

But be clear on this, my friend: God's plan to set you free is not just another self-help program. The solution is not just to "try harder" or pull yourself up by your bootstraps. No, the Lord wants to *help you*. He wants to do something *supernatural* in your life—something you're not able to do for yourself.

The Desire and the Power

Paul puts this into proper balance:

> *Work hard to show the results of your salvation, obeying God with deep reverence and fear. For God is working in you, giving you the **desire** and the **power** to do what pleases him.*
>
> (Philippians 2:12–13 NLT)

You see, God's help is the crucial ingredient in your deliverance. He not only gives you the *desire* to change, but He also gives you the *power* to change. If you've given your life to Christ, He now lives in you through the power of the Holy Spirit. (See Galatians 2:20; Colossians 1:27.) That makes all the difference.

And once you've fully surrendered to Him, you can expect the circumstances around you to change as well. Let me explain.

From a human perspective, there are many different kinds of needs you could face at one time or another. However, from God's point of view, there's only *one* thing you really need: His favor! You see, when you open your heart to God's wisdom and favor, everything else in your life is impacted. Not only will He reenergize your spiritual life, but there will be a transformation of your health, finances, and relationships as well.

That's why David could boldly say, *"Those who seek the LORD shall not lack any good thing"* (Psalm 34:10). So, in many ways, the only need you have is a *"seek the LORD"* need!

To David, this was more than a nice theory. Because he had drawn near to the Lord as his Good Shepherd, he lacked nothing. (See Psalm 23:1.) And he was so confident of God's ongoing favor in his life that he proclaimed, *"Surely your goodness and love will follow me all the days of my life, and I will dwell in the house of the LORD forever"* (verse 6 NIV).

David experienced this same kind of favor when the prophet Samuel was seeking God's direction on who Israel's next king should be. (See 1 Samuel 16.) Samuel knew the king was to be chosen from among the sons of Jesse, so he must have been puzzled when none of the seven oldest sons met with God's approval. He told Jesse: *"The LORD has not chosen these…. Are these all the sons you have?"* (verses 10–11 NIV).

Apparently no one had thought to invite David to this important gathering. He was the youngest son, and he was out tending his father's sheep.

But while everyone else was looking at factors like age and rank, God was looking for a man after His heart…who would fulfill His purposes. (See Acts 13:22, 36.)

God was looking for a person He could show His favor to!
That person can be YOU!

Friend, perhaps you feel like you're just taking care of some smelly old sheep in a forgotten place today…but tomorrow your royalty may be revealed. God's favor can change *everything*.

Brightest in the Darkness

At this point, you may want to protest, "But you don't understand. I've tried to serve the Lord faithfully for many years, yet I don't really sense His favor right now."

Believe me, I've faced similar times of struggle. Plenty of them, in fact. And so did the Bible's greatest heroes. But never forget that God's favor often shines the *brightest* amid dark days. Look at these examples:

+ **Noah** lived in an exceptionally evil generation, and the Lord was about to pour out His judgment on humanity. (See Genesis 6:1–8.) *"But Noah found favor in the eyes of the LORD"* (verse 8). What an encouraging lesson for us: Even if judgment, destruction, disease, or financial lack is all around us, we can experience God's blessings, protection, and favor.

+ **Esther** lived in extremely dangerous times, when powerful men like Haman were plotting to eradicate the Jewish people. But *"Esther found favor in the eyes of all who saw her"* (Esther 2:15 NASB). Later, that amazing favor enabled her to successfully petition the king for the Jews' safety. And just as Esther experienced, God wants to give *us* His favor *"for such a time as this"* (Esther 4:14 NASB)—so we can make an impact on the people around us.

+ **Daniel** was taken captive by the Babylonians and removed from his homeland. He could have thought the Lord had abandoned him, but instead we're told, *"God had caused the official to show favor and compassion to Daniel"* (Daniel 1:9 NIV). This is such a wonderful reminder that God's favor can come to us regardless of how difficult our circumstances seem and no matter where we are!

So, are you ready for God's favor to break through in your life? This starts with an unshakable confidence in your heavenly Father's desire to bless you and provide for you.

I also encourage you to listen for His instructions. Is there some step of faith and obedience God is asking you to take before His favor can be released?

People in the Bible often had to learn this lesson. They were asked to do such things as dip in the Jordan River, give their last bit of food to a prophet, stretch out their withered hand, wash in the pool of Siloam, or touch the hem of Jesus' garment. But whenever people exercised their faith and obeyed the Lord, He did *miracles*!

What is God asking *you* to do today? If you are waiting for Him to release His favor, He may be waiting for you to release your faith. Be expectant!

THIRTY-NINE

ACCESS YOUR UNTAPPED POTENTIAL

God showed me an important lesson several years ago when one of my relatives got her first smartphone. Before getting her fancy new iPhone, she only had a very basic cell phone that she used for making calls and occasionally sending text messages. All her friends had upgraded to iPhones, so she wanted to join them in trying out the new technology. She bought a nice blue case for it, got it all charged up, and the phone looked really pretty.

However, after having her iPhone for several years now, she still uses it for exactly the same purposes as her old flip phone—making phone calls and texting.

At one point, I gently tried to point out that she is using on a very small percentage of the phone's potential. There's so much *more* the phone could be doing for her! I patiently explained that she could have been using her phone to wake her up in the morning, show the week's weather forecast, remind her of the day's schedule, provide navigation to her appointments, keep her contacts up to date, keep track of her finances, surf the Internet, check e-mails, provide restaurant reviews, display movie show times, read her the Bible in multiple translations, play audiobooks, take pictures or videos and immediately post them to Twitter or Facebook—and much more.

Of course, all this information was totally overwhelming to her. She was just happy that the new phone worked well for phone calls and text messages.

However, this mind-set was puzzling to me. *Why buy an expensive phone and not use even close to its full potential?* It seemed like such a waste. Yet my relative was perfectly content.

I'm not sure if it's true, but I've heard that today's smartphones have more computer power than what was used to send men to the moon. Pretty amazing. Most people, then, are using so much less than the phone's actual potential.

And in exactly the same way, none of us is using more than a fraction of the incredible potential God has put in our mind and spirit.

Greater Works

As I've pondered this recently, the Lord has challenged me that I often do something far *worse* than not using the vast potential of my smartphone. Even though I'm a preacher who regularly encourages believers to stir up their faith to do the *"greater works"* Jesus promised us (John 14:12), I often fall short of this in my own life. He continues to ask me, "George, do you realize the incredible potential I've put in you by the power of the Holy Spirit?"

How convicting! When Christ lives in us by the Holy Spirit, why do we still rely so much on our own ability and ingenuity? How come we utilize such a small portion of the overwhelming power available to us?

Of course, some believers are simply ignorant of what God has made available. They're surrounded by other people who aren't tapping into the power of the Spirit either, so their Christian life seems quite "normal" to them. Like a person who has no idea of all the features available on their phone, they simply don't know what they're missing.

But I'm convinced the problem often is *spiritual laziness* rather than ignorance. Many people have *heard* about the amazing apps available for their phone, yet they refuse to take time to download the apps and learn how to use them. This isn't really very difficult, but they must *see a need* for each app and be willing to invest a little *time* to download it and put it to work.

When I fail to utilize my untapped potential, I wish I could simply claim ignorance about the power of the Holy Spirit. But I can't. I'm quite familiar with fantastic Bible promises like Philippians

4:13—*"I can do all things through Christ who strengthens me"*—I just lose sight of them at times.

If you're ever feeling weak and powerless to break loose from the hindrances in your life, I encourage you to meditate on the truth of Romans 8:11:

> *The Spirit of God, who raised Jesus from the dead, lives in you. And just as God raised Christ Jesus from the dead, he will give life to your mortal bodies by this same Spirit living within you.*
>
> (NLT)

Despite your feelings, you're not powerless at all! The same Spirit who raised Christ from the dead lives in *you!* All you need to do is recognize and tap into the incredible resurrection life that now dwells inside your mortal body.

Even the Christians in the early church sometimes neglected to utilize their full potential. That's why Paul prayed for the believers at Ephesus to see *"the exceeding greatness of His power toward us who believe, according to the working of His mighty power"* (Ephesians 1:18–19).

Today, let's pray this same prayer for each other. God has some amazing new "apps" to show us in the days ahead. We will have to tap into more of His mighty power in order to break free from mediocrity and experience a more fruitful Christian life.

FORTY

LIBERATED BY AN EARTHQUAKE

In the physical realm, earthquakes can be pretty scary. It's disconcerting to feel the ground move under your feet. But God sometimes starts earthquakes in order to set His people free.

If you want to break loose from some negative situation in your life, you may need to start an earthquake to break your chains off. I don't mean an earthquake that shakes the ground and causes the natural realm to tremble, but rather a shaking of the *spiritual* realm—demolishing satanic strongholds that are hindering God's blessings in your finances, health, or family.

This is the kind of earthquake Paul and Silas touched off in a Philippian jail in Acts 16:22–34. As they gave thanks and worshipped the Lord, *"there was a great earthquake"* that shook the prison and set the inmates free from their chains (verse 26).

After they were imprisoned, even though Paul and Silas had been brutally beaten and mistreated, they prayed, gave thanks, and sang God's praises. And the Lord responded with an earthquake that totally transformed their circumstances!

What a fantastic picture of the overwhelming *victory* God wants to give you and me as we worship and obey Him today. He will unleash a tidal wave of blessings to reverse every negative situation!

And don't miss this important fact in Acts 16:25: Paul and Silas received their breakthrough *"at midnight."* God proved Himself faithful in their darkest hour!

Friend, this is such good news. No matter what kind of difficult situation you may be facing today, your miraculous breakthrough may be closer than you think.

Thank God Before the Victory

Throughout the Bible, we see examples of God's people using *thanksgiving* and *praise* as powerful keys to overcome the enemy. In the face of seemingly impossible circumstances, God stepped in to answer His people's prayers and gave them *victory* when they gave Him *praise*.

And although it's fairly easy to thank the Lord *after* we've already received the victory, these stories teach an entirely different lesson: We must give God praise *before* we see the actual victory.

Just as God broke the chains of bondage in that jail in Philippi, He wants to break *your* chains today. As you draw near and worship Him with a thankful heart, you can be released from...

+ Poverty or debt

+ Sickness or depression

+ Loneliness or hopelessness

+ Addiction or family strife

+ And so much more!

Throughout my years of ministry, I've seen countless people set free from toxic situations that had held them back from God's best in their life. Some have found liberty from demonic oppression or an enemy stronghold. Others have miraculously received some kind of *open door* from the Lord—in a relationship, career, or ministry. As Paul and Silas passionately worshipped the Lord, *"all the doors were opened"* (verse 26).

Regardless of your situation, take a minute right now to thank the Lord. Thank Him for the victory you need, for the doors you need opened, for the answers to the prayers you've been praying. *Most of all, thank Him for His faithfulness!*

In 2 Chronicles 20, God's people were facing an impossible situation. Three different armies were coming to destroy them, and they were greatly outnumbered. Defeat seemed certain. Yet something incredible happened when they began to sing and praise the Lord. In the face of an overwhelming problem, and before they saw the victory they so desperately needed, they began to thank God for the victory. As a result, God stepped in and scattered their enemies! Remember: Your praise to God is a powerful weapon of warfare.

Just as earthquakes and tsunamis are powerful physical occurrences, your praise and worship can set off potent *spiritual* shockwaves to transform your life. Have you ever noticed that those who maintain an "attitude of gratitude" tend to attract more blessings and favor, while those who grumble and complain attract even more distress?

This shouldn't be surprising, since Paul wrote to the Philippian church that instead of being anxious, they should make their requests known to God *"with thanksgiving"* (Philippians 4:6). And he told the Thessalonians: *"In everything give thanks; for this is the will of God in Christ Jesus for you"* (1 Thessalonians 5:18).

You may have waited for a long time, but your breakthrough can come *"suddenly"* (Acts 16:26), just as it did for Paul and Silas. Even when it seems like your "midnight hour" has come, God will turn around your circumstances when you give Him praise!

This story also provides good news if you are concerned about your lost loved ones. Acts 16 says Paul and Silas started an earthquake that brought salvation not only to their jailer but to *"all his family"* (verse 33). So go ahead and boldly claim this beautiful principle: God *wants your entire family to experience His salvation and victory!*

But remember: You don't have to wait until you see the victory before you start giving God praise. Paul and Silas began to worship the Lord *before* their circumstances changed. Their worship came *first*, and then the breakthrough came.

My friend, when you cultivate a heart of thanksgiving, you will increasingly see the Lord intervene in your circumstances and give you victory. If necessary, He'll send an earthquake to set you free!

FORTY-ONE

TRUST THE LORD OF BREAKTHROUGHS

The Bible provides many different names to describe the Lord. He is our Righteousness; our Healer; our Provider; our Victory; and much more.

But one of my favorite names of God is "the Lord of Breakthroughs" or *"the Lord who bursts through"* (1 Chronicles 14:10–11 NLT). No one else in heaven or on earth can claim a powerful title such as this.

What does this mean if you are seeking a breakthrough in some area of your life today? It means there's only one place you need to look for your answer. Why? Because the closer you get to God, the closer you will be to your breakthrough.

Although this is such a simple truth, it is often overlooked. I meet so many people who are frantically seeking a breakthrough of some kind without first seeking the Lord. They need a turnaround in their finances, their health, their family, or their emotions, but they're seeking the breakthrough by their own strength and ingenuity. This approach nearly always results in frustration—not because God is unwilling to give the person a breakthrough, but because He wants them to receive it from *Him*.

King David and other biblical heroes discovered that God was the source of every blessing and breakthrough. As a shepherd, David understood that sheep cannot survive very long on their own—they need a shepherd, both to lead them to provision and to rescue them from danger. That's why he joyfully proclaimed, *"The LORD is my shepherd; I shall not want"* (Psalm 23:1).

Today the Lord of Breakthroughs is beckoning you to draw near to Him. When you do, He promises to also draw near to you: *"Draw near to God and He will draw near to you"* (James 4:8). And when you come boldly to His throne, He says you will *"find grace to help in time of need"* (Hebrews 4:16).

What resources do you need from heaven today? More love? More power? More peace? More provision? You can receive all of these things—and much more—when you draw near to the Lord of Breakthroughs.

Breakthrough by a Battle

However, the Bible also teaches that breakthroughs seldom come without a battle. In fact, the word "breakthrough" was first used as a military term to signify an offensive thrust past the defensive lines of warfare. The word entered the realm of common speech during the technological age, often used to describe a sudden discovery or invention.

God is first revealed in the Bible as the Lord of Breakthroughs in a military context involving King David. Years earlier, he had conquered the Philistine giant Goliath. But later he was preparing for battle again, facing the Philistine army not far from the site of his famous encounter with the giant.

This time, the Philistines waged their attack in the Valley of Rephaim, which means "Valley of Giants" or "Valley of Trouble." Recognizing his need for God's guidance and favor, David paused to pray, asking God for His marching orders:

> David asked God, *"Should I go out to fight the Philistines? Will you hand them over to me?"* The LORD replied, *"Yes, go ahead. I will hand them over to you."* So David and his troops went up to Baal-perazim and defeated the Philistines there. *"God did it!"* David exclaimed. *"He used me to burst through my enemies like a raging flood!"* So they named that place Baal-perazim (which means "the Lord who bursts through").
>
> (1 Chronicles 14:10–11 NLT)

The Philistines abandoned their gods and fled, but they returned again to raid the valley one more time. Even with the memory of the first victory still fresh in his mind, David prayed again and listened for the Lord's strategy:

> Once again David asked God what to do. "Do not attack them straight on," God replied. "Instead, circle around behind and attack them near the poplar trees. When you hear a sound like marching feet in the tops of the poplar trees, go out and attack! That will be the signal that God is moving ahead of you to strike down the Philistine army." So David did what God commanded, and they struck down the Philistine army all the way from Gibeon to Gezer. So David's fame spread everywhere, and the LORD caused all the nations to fear David.
>
> (1 Chronicles 14:14–17 NLT)

Notice that David did several crucial things here: He actively sought God's instructions, he listened for what the Lord would say to him, and then "David did what God commanded." And it's a good thing David was listening, for God's strategy this time required a very different approach than before.

As you seek the Lord of Breakthroughs and obey His instructions, your "Valley of Trouble" can become the very place where you have a fresh encounter with the One "who always leads us in triumph" (2 Corinthians 2:14). He will not only give you new strategies, but He will also give you new strength to carry out those strategies. (See Isaiah 40:31.)

Friend, don't despair if your victory doesn't come right away, nor be discouraged if you encounter a difficult battle before your breakthrough. And if you're struggling to shake off the memories of past failures, remember what God's Word says: "Though the righteous fall seven times, they rise again" (Proverbs 24:16 NIV).

When you fully surrender your life to the Lord of Breakthroughs, He will fight your battles. No matter how far, or how often, you may have fallen, He will lift you up and give you victory!

FORTY-TWO

CONFRONT YOUR GIANTS

The Bible is also a book about destiny—the great plan that God has for each of our lives. God promises that we can trust Him, for He wants what is best for us. *"'I know the plans that I have for you,' declares the LORD, 'plans for welfare and not for calamity, to give you a future and a hope'"* (Jeremiah 29:11 NASB).

Throughout the Bible, God assures us not only of His great love, but also of His desire to bless us so we can be a blessing to others. (See Genesis 12:2.) This is beautifully described when the Israelites are told about the wonderful land the Lord had prepared for them:

> The LORD your God is bringing you into **a good land**, a land of brooks of water, of fountains and springs, that flow out of valleys and hills; a land of wheat and barley, of vines and fig trees and pomegranates, a land of olive oil and honey; a land in which you will eat bread **without scarcity**, in which **you will lack nothing.**
>
> (Deuteronomy 8:7–9)

I don't know about you, but I would love to live in a place like God's Word describes here—a land where there's no scarcity and where I would *"lack nothing."* And I'm convinced this is still our heavenly Father's will for us!

Then why is it that so few people seem to be living this life of blessing that God offers? The main reason is that there's a battle going on! Satan is intent on fighting us every inch of the way as we pursue the Lord's destiny for our lives. Just as God has a plan for our lives, so does the devil: "*The thief comes only to steal and kill and destroy; I came that they may have life, and have it abundantly*" (John 10:10 NASB).

God's will for you is blessing and abundance. The devil's will is bondage and destruction. So which will it be? In many ways, the choice is yours. If you're like many people, your life is somewhere in between. You want God's will for your life, but you also see ways that Satan has hindered you from full obedience and victory.

The Bible declares that God has given you the tools you need to win the battle and take back what the enemy has stolen from you. The Lord wants you to live *above* your circumstances, triumphing in every area of life.

Yet in order to experience this level of victory, you must be willing to confront the "giants" blocking you from your Promised Land. Instead of putting your head in the sand and pretending everything is okay, you must be honest with God and with yourself. You must confront your fears, your sins, and your strongholds.

Your giants are whatever things you're struggling with today. Does the devil have a foothold in your marriage? Your children? Your finances? Your health? Your habits? Your emotions? God will help you to defeat any giants—but you have to get *real* with Him!

A Vision Problem

Numbers 13–14 tell a sobering story about God's desire to bring His people into the Promised Land. He instructed Moses to send out twelve spies to view the land before the rest of the Israelites entered it. After forty days, the spies returned and brought a mixed report:

> We went to the land where you sent us. It truly flows with milk and honey, and this is its fruit. Nevertheless the people who dwell in the land are strong; the cities are fortified and very large; moreover we saw the descendants of Anak there. The Amalekites dwell in the land of the South; the Hittites, the Jebusites, and the Amorites dwell in the mountains; and the Canaanites dwell by the sea and along the banks of the Jordan.   (Numbers 13:27–29)

The first ten spies reported that God had indeed given them a wonderful land of *"milk and honey"* and abundant crops. However, they saw no way that the Israelites could actually possess such a land, for it was inhabited by strong enemies and impregnable fortresses.

Perhaps this sounds a lot like your life today. You've heard about a fantastic place of victory and abundance that God has prepared for you, but the obstacles seem too great, the enemies too intimidating, and the cost too high.

Caleb and Joshua gave the people a much different report, which unfortunately was disregarded by the cowardly and unbelieving spies:

> *Then Caleb quieted the people before Moses, and said, "Let us go up at once and take possession, for* **we are well able** *to overcome it." But the men who had gone up with him said, "We are not able to go up against the people, for they are stronger than we." And they gave the children of Israel a bad report of the land which they had spied out, saying, "The land through which we have gone as spies is a land that devours its inhabitants, and all the people whom we saw in it are men of great stature. There we saw the giants (the descendants of Anak came from the giants); and we were like grasshoppers in our own sight, and so we were in their sight."* (Numbers 13:30–33)

God's people were at the very brink of the Promised Land. They were poised to enter into their destiny. Yet they allowed fear and disobedience to keep them in the wilderness for *forty more years!*

How could the ten spies get things so wrong? They gave a *"bad report"* because the obstacles to their destiny seemed like *"giants."* Is that how your problems look today—enormous and overwhelming?

The story of the ten spies who brought back a fearful and negative report provides a sobering warning for us today. Instead of cowering in fear and intimidation, we need to aggressively take the battle to the enemy. The people of God have succumbed to pacifism for too long. It's time to go on the offensive in spiritual warfare!

Passivity and accommodation never will work in warfare—whether in the physical or the spiritual realm. Jesus repeatedly spoke of the need to be on the offensive against the enemy: *"From the days of John the Baptist until now the kingdom of heaven suffers violence, and the violent take it by force"* (Matthew 11:12). We will never "take ground" from the enemy or reach our destiny without a fight!

The ten cowardly spies had a "vision" problem. They saw the obstacles (the so–called *"giants"*) as too big and God as too small. Do you see how foolish that perspective is? It will *always* rob us of obeying God and pursuing the dreams He has given us.

Whenever the Lord gives us a great "territory" to take, there will always appear to be insurmountable obstacles in the way. Unless we clearly see God as big and the problems, in comparison, as small, we will inevitably draw back and remain in the wilderness.

Unless we see God correctly...we won't have *faith.*
Unless we have faith...we won't be able to *obey.*
Without *faith* and *obedience*...we won't be able to do battle
and enter into the *destiny* God has for us.
(See Hebrews 3 and 4.)

Notice that when the Israelites saw God incorrectly, they saw *themselves* incorrectly as well. The ten fainthearted spies saw themselves and their countrymen as mere *"grasshoppers"* in comparison to the enemy *"giants"* in the Promised Land. Just two of the spies, Joshua and Caleb, saw God.

What do *you* see when you look around you today? Lots of believers are still locked in the "Grasshopper Syndrome," failing to see who they are in Christ. Sure, the problems we face may be bigger than *us.* But they definitely aren't bigger than our Lord!

Confidence in the Strength of Our Lord

Joshua defeated the enemy kings not because of his own military power, but *"because the LORD God of Israel fought for Israel"* (Joshua 10:42). At the end of Joshua's life, God told the Israelites that their victories had come because of His supernatural help, *"not with your sword or with your bow"* (Joshua 24:12).

Look at the abundant success Joshua and his warriors later experienced: *"**Not one** of all their enemies had withstood them, for the LORD had given **all** their enemies into their hands"* (Joshua 21:44 ESV). How would you like to have that kind of testimony today—victory over *all* your enemies?

It's important to realize that Joshua's experience wasn't just a fluke, based on some kind of unique gift or favor in his life. When we take a stand based on our covenant relationship with God and our position in Christ, we are promised this same kind of overwhelming success:

> *What then shall we say to these things? If God is for us, who can be against us?*   (Romans 8:31 ESV)

> *In all these things we are more than conquerors through him who loved us.*   (Romans 8:37 ESV)

> *Thanks be to God who always leads us in triumph in Christ, and manifests through us the sweet aroma of the knowledge of Him in every place.*   (2 Corinthians 2:14 NASB)

It's clear from these Scriptures that in Christ we are a lot more than just "grasshoppers"! When we learn to use His name to wage war for our destiny, we become mighty warriors.

Whatever your giant may be, you can be encouraged by the story of David's battle with Goliath. In David's case, it wasn't just a *figurative* giant, it was a *real* one! Goliath was nearly ten feet tall—probably almost *twice* the size of David. If anyone could have justifiably felt the size of a grasshopper, it would have been David. Yet that wasn't his mind-set at all. His eyes weren't on his own size or the size of his enemy, but rather on the size of his God!

How could David face such an imposing enemy with confidence? Because his confidence wasn't in his own strength, but the strength of the Lord. When taunted by his massive enemy, David boldly replied: *"The battle is the LORD's and He will give you into our hands"* (1 Samuel 17:47 NASB).

David later wrote a song about God's faithfulness in giving him victory when he confronted his giants: *"Through God we shall do valiantly, and it is He who will tread down our adversaries"* (Psalm 60:12 NASB). Yes, spiritual adversaries will come, but God has given us the power to crush Satan's forces under our feet.

Remember, my friend: If you belong to Christ today, your battle is the Lord's. Don't let any Goliath intimidate you and keep you back from your destiny. It's time to go in and possess your Promised Land!

FORTY-THREE

HOW YOUR FAMILY CAN BREAK LOOSE

The focus of this book is primarily how you as an *individual* can break free from the things that have been keeping you from God's best for your life. But the Lord cares about your loved ones too. He wants each member of your family to break loose of any old patterns of dysfunction, addiction, or abuse.

The truth of the matter is that Satan doesn't always attack us head-on. He knows it's often more effective to launch his fiery darts toward those we love—whether that means our children, our grand-children, or our spouse. Nothing is more painful than watching our loved ones suffer from the devil's attacks or their own wrong choices.

Fighting for the Family

Christian families are under attack today! The devil is success-fully pitting many husbands and wives against each other, and many children against their parents. There's a spiritual battle going on, and we can't be passive. We must *fight*!

> Remember the Lord who is great and awesome, and **fight** for your brothers, your sons, your daughters, your wives and your houses. (Nehemiah 4:14 NASB)

Thankfully, God has already promised to turn people's hearts to Him and to each other:

> Before the coming of the great and dreadful day of the LORD.... **He will turn the hearts** of the fathers to the children, and the

*hearts of the children to their fathers, lest I come and strike the
earth with a curse.*   (Malachi 4:5–6)

This is a powerful promise for each of us to claim for our families. If this doesn't happen, the result is pretty dismal: God will "*strike
the earth with a curse.*"

However, God has a plan to turn things around, both for you and
for your family. You can be confident He will faithfully answer your
prayers for your loved ones, even if they're presently "*afar off*": "*The
promise is to you and to your **children**, and to all who are **afar off**…*"
(Acts 2:39).

Of course, winning the hearts of your loved ones will require
not only your prayers, but your godly example as well. Proverbs 22:6
promises, "*Train up a child in the way he should go, and when he is old he
will not depart from it.*" This certainly doesn't mean you must be perfect, but you need to recognize that your life will inevitably have an
impact, either positive or negative, on those around you. That's one of
the reasons it's so crucial for you to break free in your own life. That's
the only way you'll be able to successfully influence others.

Joshua knew that his decisions would affect not only his own
life, but also his family: "*As for me and my house, we will serve the
LORD*" (Joshua 24:15). Because he himself had determined to follow
the Lord wholeheartedly, he trusted that his family would ultimately
do likewise.

So what can you do if you have family members who aren't presently walking with the Lord? I encourage you to lay hold of the numerous promises of God's Word. For example, when the Philippian jailer
asked Paul and Silas what he had to do in order to be saved, they
replied, "*Believe on the Lord Jesus Christ, and **you will be saved, you
and your household***" (Acts 16:31).

What a beautiful promise about God's desire to transform not
only *your* life, but the lives of your entire family. So if your loved ones
are presently bound by Satan's snares, don't give up. Keep interceding

and doing spiritual battle against the enemy. God wants your whole household to be saved and set free.

Perhaps you've heard the story of a widow named Monica, who wrestled in prayer for many years for the salvation of her wayward son. It seemed that the more she prayed, the worse his situation became. He lived in blatant immorality and even spent several years in a cult. Despite her efforts to share the gospel with him, his heart seemed completely hardened.

Finally, at age thirty-three, Monica's son was converted and baptized. The son, who became known as Saint Augustine, became one of the most influential theologians in church history. Monica went to be with the Lord shortly after Augustine's conversion, but God had been faithful to answer her prayers.

Claim His Promises

On a regular basis, I run into men and women who want me to intercede for a breakthrough of some kind in their family. This shouldn't really be surprising, since many of Jesus' miracles were in direct response to the pleas of desperate people who sought His help for their children and loved ones. Here are just a few examples:

+ Healing Jairus's daughter (Mark 5:22–43)

+ Casting a demon out of a mute boy (Mark 9:17–29)

+ Healing a nobleman's dying son (John 4:46–53)

+ Healing the demon-possessed daughter of a Gentile woman (Matthew 15:21–28)

+ Resurrecting the son of the widow of Nain (Luke 7:11–15)

These stories contain a wonderful message for us today: God delights in answering our fervent prayers for our children and family members. Whatever difficult situations your loved ones face—sickness, sin, rebellion, depression, or addiction—the Lord wants you to confidently bring your intercessions to Him. Through your prayers and godly example, you can impact your entire family and leave a powerful legacy.

God is faithful, and He will help you not only win your own spiritual battles, but also bring deliverance and victory to your loved ones. He is able to transform even the hardest heart or most difficult circumstances. *Nothing* is too difficult for Him. (See Jeremiah 32:17.)

God loves you more than you can comprehend, and you never need to doubt His concern for you, your spouse, your children, or your grandchildren. When you entrust your family into His hands, you can be filled with joy and peace—*regardless* of your present circumstances.

Amid the battles your family may face along the way, take time to read God's Word and claim His promises for your family. In the pages of Scripture, you'll find divine help to strengthen your faith, provide courage, impart wisdom, and offer reassurance that the Lord truly *can* break through in the lives of your loved ones.

Remember: God has not planned defeat for you or your family. As difficult as your situation may be, with God there is always a way, for He is our Way-Maker and the Healer of our hearts.

FORTY-FOUR

VICTORY WHEN YOU FEEL OVERWHELMED

If you're anything like me, some days you feel like you're conquering the world—and other days the world seems to be conquering *you*. Although I usually respond pretty well when confronted with just one problem at a time, it's overwhelming when the problems come at me from every side. Some days I feel like I'm playing a game of cosmic Whack-a-Mole, with troubles springing up everywhere.

Yet I'm comforted to know that many others have written about days when they were surrounded by problems on every side. I want to look at one incredible example: King Jehoshaphat.

King Jehoshaphat, likewise, felt overwhelmed when *"a great multitude"* of enemies surrounded him (2 Chronicles 20:2). I encourage you to read the entire story for yourself, but here are a few of the key tips for experiencing victory when problems attack you from every direction:

1. Recognize that God is bigger than your problems.

When facing overwhelming situations, it's easy to feel quite small and vulnerable, if not hopeless. But look at how Jehoshaphat focused on God's power and sovereignty, rather than trying to defeat the enemies in his own strength: *"O Lord God of our fathers, are You not God in heaven, and do You not rule over all the kingdoms of the nations, and in Your hand is there not power and might, so that no one is able to withstand You?"* (verse 6).

2. Reflect on God's past faithfulness.

If you've been walking with the Lord for a while, you hopefully have many memories of how He came to your aid during past battles. Jehoshaphat called to mind stories of God's past miracles and promises, and he prayed, *"Are You not our God, who drove out the inhabitants of this land before Your people Israel, and gave it to the descendants of Abraham Your friend forever?"* (verse 7).

3. Rely on God's power rather than your own.

In crisis situations, there's often a temptation to "take matters into your own hands" rather than trust the Lord and ask for His strategies. But Jehoshaphat freely acknowledged that he was powerless to handle things without God's intervention: *"We have no power against this great multitude that is coming against us; nor do we know what to do, but our eyes are upon You"* (verse 12). Notice that Jehoshaphat made a conscious decision to fix his eyes on the Lord instead of on his problems. (See, for example, Hebrews 12:2.)

4. Cast aside all fear.

In a crisis, you need faith. Fear is never your friend. While Jehoshaphat was praying about his dire situation, the Spirit of God spoke an encouraging prophetic word to banish his fears: *"Do not be afraid nor dismayed because of this great multitude, for the battle is not yours, but God's"* (verse 15). You see, if the battle is *yours*, it's quite reasonable for you to feel afraid. But when you realize that God is fighting on your behalf, victory is assured, and there's no need to fear.

5. Listen for God's strategy.

Yes, the Lord will fight our battles, but victory comes only when we listen for, and obey, His strategy for our situation. In the case of this battle faced by the people of Judah, God's strategy was to send a team of *worshippers* before the army: *"When they began to sing and to praise, the* LORD *set ambushes against the people of Ammon, Moab, and Mount Seir, who had come against Judah; and they were defeated"* (verse 22). In times of trouble, praise is a powerful weapon, both to calm our hearts and to release God's intervention.

6. Look for the *blessings* amid the *battles*.

In this remarkable story, the Lord not only caused Jehoshaphat's enemies to destroy each other, but the end result was a huge treasure trove of plunder: *"When Jehoshaphat and his people came to take away their spoil, they found among them an abundance of valuables on the dead bodies, and precious jewelry, which they stripped off for themselves, more than they could carry away"* (verse 25). When first surrounded by enemy armies, Jehoshaphat probably would have considered it a great victory just to *survive* the battle. But God has much *more* in mind. He wanted Jehoshaphat and his people to *thrive*, becoming far better off *after* the encounter than before. If you're going through a difficult trial today, remember that God can use it to give you far greater blessings in the end than in the beginning.

7. Enter into God's rest, even if the battle is still raging all around you.

The story ends with this beautiful conclusion: *"Then the realm of Jehoshaphat was quiet, for his God gave him rest all around"* (verse 30). If your battles have been intense and long-lasting, it may be difficult to envision finding a time of peace and security ever again. But God wants to give *your* story a happy ending, just as He did for Jehoshaphat.

Jesus predicted we would face some pretty overwhelming times in the last days, so we shouldn't be surprised when that happens. His advice was simple, though. Instead of focusing on our surrounding circumstances, He told us, *"Look up and lift up your heads, because your redemption draws near"* (Luke 21:28).

The Message paraphrases it this way: *"When all this starts to happen, up on your feet. Stand tall with your heads high. Help is on the way!"* So take courage, my friend. When you look up and turn your eyes upon Jesus, you can be sure that help is on the way.

FORTY-FIVE

WHAT'S STILL HOLDING YOU BACK?

In chapter after chapter, I've shared about God's desire to set you free from anything that is hindering you from His best. Hopefully you've already gained a new level of freedom and victory, but I want to probe a little further and see if you have any remaining issues that are holding you back.

As you pray for God's intervention in your circumstances, make sure you're also listening to His instructions on what you're to *do*. Sometimes we're waiting on God to deliver us from some kind of difficult situation, when He's waiting on us to obey the voice of His Spirit and take *action*.

The Bible is full of examples of people who received a breakthrough only *after* they took a step of faith: a geographical move, an act of forgiveness and reconciliation, a season of prayer and fasting, or surrendering something to the Lord that they'd been hanging onto. For example, Naaman had to dip seven times in the Jordan, the woman with the hemorrhage had to touch Jesus' cloak, and Job needed to pray for his friends, before healing came.

As we reach the end of this book, take a few minutes to examine your life in light of these biblical examples of men and women, some of whom we've met before, who exercised their faith for God's breakthroughs, not allowing anything to hold them back.

If people or geography have held you back from your highest calling in the Lord…

Remember **Abraham**, who at age seventy-five was called by God to leave his relatives and the idolatrous culture of Ur in order to venture out to a Promised Land that the Lord had prepared for him and his descendants. (See Genesis 12:1–4.)

If you've been victimized and mistreated, causing you physical or emotional trauma...

Remember **Joseph**, who forgave his jealous brothers even though they had thrown him into a well and sold him into slavery. (See Genesis 50:18–21.)

Remember the **woman at the well** (see John 4:1–42) and the **woman caught in adultery** (see John 8:1–11), who both were traumatized at the hands of men and their own foolish choices—yet they each received a life-changing turnaround when Jesus forgave and restored them.

If you've been ridiculed, rejected, or labeled as "a pain"...

Remember **Jabez**, who overcame a difficult childhood by crying out to God for a breakthrough of prosperity and blessing. (See 1 Chronicles 4:9–10.)

If you've suffered the grief and pain of losing a loved one...

Remember **Naomi** and **Ruth**, who found a wonderful new beginning when they moved back to Judah after the deaths of their husbands. (See Ruth 1:1–22.)

If you've committed immorality or an act of violence against another person...

Remember **David**, who received God's forgiveness and cleansing after committing adultery with Bathsheba and murdering her husband, Uriah. (See Psalm 51, Psalm 32:1–5.)

If you're facing insurmountable financial struggles...

Remember the **widow at Zarephath**, who found God's supernatural provision when she sacrificially provided for Elijah despite her own needs. (See 1 Kings 17:8–16.)

If you're facing a serious illness...

Remember **Naaman**, the Syrian general who was healed of leprosy when he obeyed the prophet Elisha's instructions and dipped seven times in the Jordan River. (See 2 Kings 5:1–27.)

Remember **King Hezekiah**, whose life was extended by fifteen years when he seemed to be on his deathbed. (See 2 Kings 20:1–6.)

Remember the **woman with a hemorrhage**, who suffered for twelve years before receiving a supernatural healing when she touched the hem of Jesus' garment. (See Mark 5:25–34.)

If you've been bound by fear, depression, or some other form of oppression from the enemy…

Remember how Jesus set the **Gerasene demoniac** free from Satan's bondage into glorious liberty. (See Mark 5:1–20.)

If you've allowed fear and cowardice to cause you to deny your relationship with the Lord…

Remember **Peter**, who denied the Lord three times yet received a new beginning of leadership and fruitfulness in God's kingdom. (See John 21:15–17.)

If you've been religious, but realize you lack an intimate relationship with the Lord…

Remember **Nicodemus**, who learned that he needed to be born again spiritually, so he could see and enter into the kingdom. (See John 3:1–8.)

Remember **Saul of Tarsus**, who was zealously persecuting Christians until he was dramatically converted on the road to Damascus. (See Acts 9:1–19, Philippians 3:3–11.)

If you've strayed from God and squandered your life in wild living and addiction…

Remember the **Prodigal Son**, who experienced a turnaround and fresh favor when he made a decision to return to his father's house. (See Luke 15:11–32.)

All these people—and many more—received breakthroughs from God when they *believed* Him and took steps to *obey* His instructions. They were just ordinary people who cried out to an extraordinary God. And He heard their prayers!

As you are sensitive to the voice of God's Spirit, He will show you the steps of faith *you* need to take in order for your breakthrough to begin. Don't procrastinate. Don't make excuses or blame others for the difficult circumstances you face. And don't give up on receiving the breakthrough you need from God.

Remember: You have a heavenly Father who loves you deeply. He has a fantastic plan for your life. (See Jeremiah 29:11.) He wants to empower you with His Holy Spirit and give you every resource you need for an abundant life in Christ. (See John 10:10.)

Not only will God be faithful to give you a turnaround in your circumstances, but He will also be faithful to *continue* that work of transformation in the days, weeks, months, and years ahead. My friend, you can hold on to God's wonderful promise in Philippians 1:6:

He who began a good work in you will be faithful to complete it!

BISHOP BLOOMER'S
SPIRITUAL WARFARE DICTIONARY

Abyss: A large, gaping, unending hole characterized by darkness and powerlessness; a place of punishment for demons, enemies, and others who would do you harm and block you from your purpose and destiny. (See Luke 8:31; Revelation 9:1–2, 11; 11:7; 17:8; 20:1–3.)

adversary: A person, group, or force that opposes or attacks; an enemy; a foe; someone who contends with or is combative against another; an opponent. Chiefly, Satan. (See Exodus 23:22; 1 Kings 5:4; Amos 3:11; Matthew 5:25; 1 Peter 5:8.)

ambush: The act of waiting in a concealed position in order to launch a surprise attack; a surprise attack from such a position; the concealed position from which such an attack is launched; the person or persons waiting to launch such an attack. (See 2 Chronicles 20:21–23.)

antichrist: A particular personage or power, variously identified or explained, who is conceived of as appearing in the world as the principal antagonist of Christ; an opponent of Christ; a person, spirit, or power antagonistic to Christ. (See 1 John 2:18; 4:3.)

angels: Spiritual beings, messengers, ministers, and givers of instructions, guidance, direction, interpreted dreams, guard, and destruction. (See Luke 1:11–38; Revelation 10:1; 14:15–20; 19:17.)

    a.   A strong angel. (See Revelation 5:2.)

    b.   The four angels who stood on the four corners of the earth. (See Revelation 7:1.)

c.   The angel ascending from the east, having the seal of the living God. (See Daniel 8:16; 9:21; Revelation 7:2.)

d.   Angel as guard. (See Matthew 26:53; Luke 4:10; Jude 1:5–7.)

e.   Musical angels. (See Revelation 8:1–13.)

f.   Agent of destruction. (See Revelation 8:14–18; 15:1, 8.)

anoint: To smear or rub with oil or an oily substance, or to apply oil as a sacrament especially for consecration. It also means to choose by divine election. (See Exodus 40:9; 1 Samuel 16:1–13; Luke 4:18.)

anointing: Divine empowerment to accomplish God's will and purpose, advancing His kingdom upon the earth. (See Luke 4:18.)

apostle: One sent forth by commission to plow out new territory for the purpose of ministry in fulfillment of the Great Commission. (See Matthew 10:2; Ephesians 2:20; 4:11–12.)

archangel: A chief angel; a celestial being; intermediary agent between God and man. (See Daniel 10; 1 Thessalonians 4:16–17; Jude 1:9; Revelation 12:7–9.)

armor: Protective covering used to prevent damage from being inflicted to an individual or a vehicle through use of direct contact weapons or projectiles, usually during combat; spiritual protection from God via salvation, faith, the gospel, righteousness, truth, peace, and His Word; the whole armor of God includes the shield of faith, helmet of salvation, breastplate of righteousness, belt of truth, battle shoes, sword of the Spirit, and praying in the Spirit. (See 1 Samuel 14:1, 6; 17:6, 38–39, 54; 18:4; 31:9–10; 2 Samuel 2:21; 18:15; 20:8; 1 Kings 10:25; 20:11; 22:34; 1 Chronicles 10:9–10; 2 Chronicles 9:24; 18:33; 26:14; Nehemiah 4:16; Isaiah 22:8; 45:1; Jeremiah 46:4; 51:3; Luke 11:22; Romans 13:12; 2 Corinthians 6:7; Ephesians 6:10–17.)

arsenal: A place of storage containing arms and military equipment for land or naval service; a government establishment where military munitions are manufactured; a collection or supply of weapons. (See Jeremiah 50:24–26.)

atheism: From the Greek word *atheos*, which means "without gods." An atheist is someone who doesn't believe in any gods. (See Psalm 14:1, compare with Acts 17:22–23.)

attraction: In the spiritual warfare context, a desire or pull toward a temptation or sin. (See Leviticus 18:22–30; 20:13.)

authority: The power to influence or command thoughts, opinions, or behaviors. (See John 1:12; Colossians 2:9–11; 1 Peter 3:22.)

aura: Subtle but distinctive and pervasive quality or character emanating from a person, place, or thing; a distinctive atmosphere perceived as surrounding a given source. (See Judges 6:22; Ecclesiastes 1:17; Matthew 22:18; Mark 2:8; Luke 1:22; 5:22.)

battle: A military encounter or confrontation with Satan and the powers of darkness. (See 2 Chronicles 32:8; Ephesians 6:10–13.)

Beast: There are two Beasts described in the Scriptures. The first Beast comes out of the sea, having seven heads and ten horns. The second Beast comes out of the earth, having the disguise of a lamb, while speaking as a dragon. This Beast will exercise authority on behalf of the first beast, causing the earth-dwellers to make an image of the first Beast and worship it. It is able to give life to this image so that it can speak and kill anyone who doesn't worship the first Beast. (See Revelation 13.)

Beelzebub: The prince of devils. Latin and Greek words were derived from Hebrew *Baal zĕbhûbh*, a Philistine god, literally meaning Lord of the Flies, God of Ekron, or Lord of Dung. The fact that Beelzebub is "the prince of the demons" implies that he has a kingdom. (See 2 Kings 1:3, 6, 16; Matthew 10:25; 12:24, 27; Mark 3:22; Luke 11:15–19.)

bishop: A spiritual overseer of a movement or area of ministry. A pastor of pastors, a director or head superintendent. (See 1 Timothy 3:11; Titus 1:7.)

blessing: Something beneficial, providing advantage, avail, benefit, boon, favor, gain, or profit; the act or words of a person who blesses; a special favor, mercy, or benefit: e.g., the blessing of liberty; a favor or gift bestowed by God, thereby bringing happiness; the invoking of God's favor upon a person or activity; praise; devotion; worship, such as grace said before a meal; approval or good wishes. (See Genesis 49:25–26; Deuteronomy 28:2; Joshua 8:34; Psalm 21:3; Proverbs 10:6; 28:20; Malachi 2:2.)

bondage: An attachment to a sin from which it is metaphorically difficult to free oneself; the power of physical corruption as against the freedom of life; the power of fear as against the confidence of Christian faith; bondage to the letter of the Law or religious rituals, rather than a true relationship with God through Jesus Christ. There can be various levels of bondage, from the mild (that which with some effort a person can free himself) to the severe (that which requires intervention from a third party). (See Romans 8:15, 21; Hebrews 2:15.)

born again: Supernatural inner spiritual renewal and conversion as a result of God's power in a person's life. (See John 3:7.)

bottomless pit: A large, gaping, unending hole characterized by darkness and powerlessness; a symbol of hopelessness, despair, defeat, and torment. (See Revelation 9:1; 17:8; 20:1.)

bound: Tied up; taken captive in bonds; held or tied to another element, substance, or material in a physical, spiritual, or emotional union. (See Matthew 14:3; Mark 5:4; Luke 8:29; 10:34; John 11:44.)

breastplate: Device worn over the torso that protects from injury; item of religious significance; an ornament covering the breast of the high priest, made of embroidered cloth, set with four rows of precious stones, three in each row, and on each stone was engraved the name of one of the twelve tribes. (See Exodus 25:7; 28:15–29; 39:8–21; Isaiah 59:17; Ephesians 6:14.)

bureaucracy: A system of policies, procedures, and guidelines that are characterized by layers of processes that are difficult to navigate; levels of challenges and opposition to be passed or overthrown in order to receive approval, blessings, and promotion. (See 1 Samuel 8:10–18; Ecclesiastes 5:18.)

calling: An inner urge or a strong impulse, especially one believed to be divinely inspired, to accept the Gospels as truth and Jesus as one's personal Savior; an occupation, profession, or career inspired by God's leading. (See Matthew 20:16; 22:14; 2 Peter 1:10.)

confession: Acknowledgment, avowal, admission of sin before God. (See 1 John 1:9; Romans 10:9–10.)

captivity: To be imprisoned, enslaved, or confined; held under control of another but having the appearance of independence. (See Romans 7:23; 2 Corinthians 10:5; Ephesians 4:8.)

carnal: Pertaining to or characterized by the flesh or the body, its passions and appetites; sensual; worldly; unspiritual. (See 2 Corinthians 10:3–5; Ephesians 6:12.)

cast out: To banish, eject, exile, expel, ostracize, oust; e.g., to cast out or exorcise evil spirits. (See Mark 9:26.)

cherubim: Guardians attached to the throne of God as a protective barrier to guard His holiness, and to the garden of Eden to guard the Tree of Life. (See Genesis 3:27; Ezekiel 1:5–12; 10:1–22; Isaiah 37:16; Hebrews 12:22.)

compartments of hell: Tartarus, Abraham's Bosom, hades or Sheol, the Abyss, the lake of fire.

a. Tartarus: A Greek word describing hell. The compartment where fallen angels are kept, reserved in chains of darkness until they are judged by God and cast into the final hell, the lake of fire. (See 2 Peter 2:4; Jude 1:6.)

b. Abraham's Bosom (the paradise of old): The compartment where all the righteous dead of the Old Testament were kept. There was no torment or suffering in Abraham's Bosom. It was simply a place of holding until the death and resurrection of Jesus. Jesus paid the price of redemption by shedding His blood. At the resurrection of Jesus, Abraham's Bosom was emptied and removed from the heart of the earth and is now located in heaven. All the captives were set free and resurrected. (See Matthew 27:51–53; Luke 16:19–31.)

c. Hades or Sheol: The place where the wicked were kept after death. When the sinner dies, his spirit and soul go immediately to this place of torment. Hades is the place (or state) of departed souls; the grave; hell. Because the word *grave* is mentioned in the definition of hades, it is said by some that hell is the common grave; and from this, the erroneous doctrine of soul sleep is derived. But note that the rich man of Luke 16 was in hades, and his soul was clearly not asleep. Rather, his soul was in much turmoil. The term *Sheol* is the Hebrew word for *hades* or *hell*, the world of the dead, its accessories and inmates, or simply the grave or pit. (See Psalm 9:17; Isaiah 14:9; Luke 16:23; Revelation 20:13.)

d. The Abyss (bottomless pit): This compartment of hell is where Satan will be bound for 1,000 years during the millennial reign of Christ on earth. Also, during the time of the Great Tribulation period, it will be where the locust-like scorpion creatures will come and torment mankind for five months. The Abyss will not be the eternal home of Satan. He will be loosed from this prison to be judged and then cast into the eternal hell, the lake of fire. (See Revelation 9:1–11; 20:1–7, 10.)

e. The lake of fire (Greek *Gehenna*): The eternal home of all sin and rebellion. At the close of the White Throne Judgment, this will be the home of the wicked, those who rebelled against God. Fallen humanity will reside there for all eternity to suffer the pains of an eternal hell. Satan will be there for all eternity to suffer also. According to the Scriptures, Satan will be tormented day and night, forever and ever, having no rest. Also, hades and Sheol will be cast into the eternal hell. Those who inhabit hades and Sheol will be resurrected to face God's judgment and then cast into the lake of fire. In the very end of God's judgments, Satan, fallen angels, the wicked, and sin will all have their home in the lake of fire. (See Revelation 20:11–15.)

conflict: Competitive or opposing action between incompatibles; antagonistic state or action (as of divergent ideas, interests, or persons); mental struggle resulting from incompatible or opposing needs, drives, wishes, or external or internal demands; the state of constant antagonism between the forces of good and the forces of evil. (See Galatians 5:17.)

confront: To face in hostility or defiance; oppose; to bring together for examination or comparison; to stand, come in front of, or meet facing. (See Exodus 8:20; Judges 14:4; 1 Samuel 12:6–7; 2 Samuel 22:19; Isaiah 50:8.)

confusion: A state of being bewildered or misled; lack of peace or clarity. (See 1 Corinthians 14:33; Acts 19:29.)

conquer: To acquire by force or arms; to subdue; to surmount, master, or overcome. (See Genesis 14:7; Numbers 24:18; Deuteronomy 2:31; Joshua 10:42; 12:6–7; 23:4; Hebrews 11:33; Revelation 13:7.)

consecration: The devoting or setting apart of anything to the worship or service of God. (See Exodus 28:3; 29:22, 26–27, 31, 33–34; Leviticus 7:37; 8:22, 28–29, 31, 33.)

counsel: Advice; opinion or instruction given in directing the judgment or conduct of another; interchange of opinions as to future procedures or actions; consultation; deliberation; a private or secret opinion or purpose; to get or take counsel or advice. (See Proverbs 11:14.)

covenant: An agreement, usually formal, between two or more persons to do or not do something specified; a solemn agreement between the members of a church to act together in harmony with the precepts of the gospel; the conditional promises made to humanity by God, as revealed in Scripture. (See Genesis 6:18; 9:13–15.)

crown: A band encircling the head by way of honor; the royal badge of kings; the sacerdotal badge of priests; the prize winner's badge of victory; in Greek, *diadeema*, "diadem," which KJV translates as *"crown"* in Revelation 12:3; in Revelation 19:12 it is restricted to Christ the King of kings; Satan wears it only as usurping Christ's right. (See Revelation 13:1.)

curses: To call out negative supernatural power in order to cause or create injury upon another person or a situation; to invoke evil; to execrate; to utter negativities; to affirm the negative or deny the positive; to harass or torment; to pray for harm or injury; malediction; the cause of harm; punishment from God because of disobedience. (See Deuteronomy 28:45.)

deception: Misleading by a false appearance or statement; to falsely persuade others; the practice of deceit. (See Psalm 5:6; 12:2; 38:12; Ecclesiastes 7:26; Jeremiah 17:9; 2 Corinthians 4:2; Romans 3:13.)

declare: To make known formally, officially, or explicitly; to make evident; to state emphatically. (See Exodus 4:31; Isaiah 28:5–6; 30:18–26; John 8:26, 28; 12:49–50; 14:10, 24; 15:15; 17:8, 26; Acts 15:12.)

deliverance: A thought or judgment expressed; an authoritative pronouncement; salvation; protection from the power of another (person, place, thing or idea); to take (as a prisoner) forcibly from custody. (See 2 Kings 13:17; 1 Chronicles 11:14; Obadiah 17; Luke 4:18.) The first step to deliverance is actually believing that any Christian can have or be influenced by a demon, even a born-again, Spirit-filled, tongue-talking, Jesus-loving, worshipping Christian. Jesus said that deliverance is the *"children's bread."* (See Matthew 15:26; Mark 7:27.)

demons: Disembodied spirits that influence or take possession of human bodies; fallen angels that joined Satan in the rebellion against God and were subsequently cast down. Their original habitation was in heaven, where they served as angels. They now temporarily inhabit the unseen spiritual realm. (See Matthew 25:41; Luke 10:17; James 2:19; Jude 6; Revelation 12:4–9.)

demonic possession: Domination by something (as an evil spirit, a passion, or an idea); a psychological state in which an individual's normal personality is replaced by another. (See Matthew 8:28–34; Mark 1:21–28; 9:14–29; Acts 16:16–18; Ephesians 6:10–18.)

demonization: To make subject to the influence or control of a demon; to characterize or conceive of as evil, cruel, inhuman, etc.;

to bring under the influence of demons. (See Matthew 4:24; 17:15; Luke 4:33; 6:18; 8:29; 9:42; 11:24.)

demonstration: The act or circumstance of conclusive proof by a show of evidence; a description or explanation; a public display or manifestation. (See 1 Corinthians 2:4; Romans 5:8.)

destiny: Something that is meant to happen or has happened to a particular person or thing; lot or fortune; the predetermined, usu-ally inevitable or irresistible, course of events; a predetermined course of events considered as something beyond human power or control. (See Jeremiah 1:5; 29:11; Matthew 4:29; Ephesians 1:3–5.)

devil: God's enemy; Satan, who rules hell and tempts people to sin. (See Job 1:6; Zechariah 3:1; Revelation 2:10; 12:10.)

device: A plan or scheme for effecting a purpose; a trick. (See 2 Corinthians 2:11.)

discernment: The quality of being able to grasp and comprehend what is obscure; to detect with the eyes; to detect with senses other than vision; to be cognizant of the spiritual world. (See 1 Corinthians 12:10.)

discipline: Training expected to produce a specific character or pat-tern of behavior, especially training that produces moral or mental improvement; controlled behavior resulting from disciplinary train-ing; self-control; a set of rules or methods, as those regulating the practice of a church or monastic order; to train by instruction and practice, especially to teach self-control. (See Psalm 1:1–3, 46:10, 119:72; Proverbs 22:6.)

discord: Strife; dispute; vigorous or bitter conflict. (See Proverbs 6:14, 19; Galatians 5:20.)

dispensation: The divine ordering of the affairs of the world; a divinely appointed order or age; a religious system or code of com-mands considered to have been divinely revealed or appointed. (See Ephesians 1:10; 3:2; Colossians 1:25.)

distraction: Disarrangement; disorder; something that divides the attention; that which amuses, entertains, and diverts in order to pre-vent concentration; mental confusion. (See 1 Corinthians 7:35.)

divination: The practice of attempting to foretell future events or discover hidden knowledge by occult or supernatural means. (See Deuteronomy 18:10; Acts 16:16–18.)

doctrine: A particular principle, position, or policy taught or advocated; a body or system of teachings relating to a particular subject, e.g., the doctrine of Original Sin. (See Proverbs 4:2; Matthew 16:12; Ephesians 4:14; Titus 1:9; 2 John 1:9–10; Revelation 2:24.)

doubt: To be uncertain about; to consider something questionable or unlikely; to hesitate to believe; to distrust; to be undecided in opinion or belief. (See Genesis 3:1; Matthew 4:3, 6; Luke 4:3, 9.)

domain: A territory or region over which dominion is exercised. Within a domain exists kingdoms. The word *kingdom* is derived from the words "king" and "domain." Thus a kingdom is the king's domain, the region over which he exercises absolute rule, power, and authority. Scripture teaches that God created all things and without Him nothing was made that was made. Therefore, by virtue of creation, God's domain is all-expansive, all-inclusive, and indefinite. He established His throne in heaven, and His kingdom rules over all. (See Genesis 1:26–28; Psalm 103:19; 115:15–17; John 1:3.)

dominion: Supreme authority or control; sovereignty; a territory or sphere of control or influence; realm. (See Genesis 1:26; Judges 5:13; Daniel 7:27.)

dream: A sequence of images that appear involuntarily to the mind of somebody who is sleeping, often a mixture of real and imaginary characters, places, and events; a series of images, usually pleasant ones that pass through the mind of somebody who is awake; an involuntary vision occurring to a person when awake; a vision voluntarily indulged in while awake; something hoped for or that somebody hopes, longs, or is ambitious for, usually something difficult to attain or far removed from present circumstances; an aspiration, goal, or aim. (See Genesis 37:5–10, 41; Numbers 12:6; Job 33:15; Hosea 12:10; Matthew 2:12–13; Acts 2:17.)

dry places: Uninhabitable domains occupied by demons and unclean spirits; in Scripture, the Word of God is likened to water, and just as water in the natural sense is imperative to life, so is God and His Word. (See Luke 11:24; John 3:14.)

enchanter: One who casts spells over an individual or thing; one who bewitches. (See Deuteronomy 18:10; Jeremiah 27:9.)

enemy: A person who feels hatred for, fosters harmful designs against, or engages in antagonistic activities against another; an adversary or opponent; sometimes used to connote the devil. (See 1 Peter 5:8.)

error: Belief in something untrue; a moral offense; wrongdoing. (See Job 19:4; Isaiah 32:6; Matthew 22:29; 1 Thessalonians 2:3.)

eschatology: Any system of doctrine concerning last, or final, matters, such as death, the final judgment, or the future state; the branch of theology dealing with such matters. (See 1 Timothy 4:1–3.)

eternity: Having no end or limit; immeasurable; without boundaries; time without beginning or end in the afterlife. (See Isaiah 57:15.)

evangelist: Someone who shares the gospel of Jesus Christ; a mission preacher responsible for making way for a jurisdiction preacher. (See Ephesians 4:11.)

exorcism: The practice of purging demons, evil ghosts, dark influences, malevolent spirits, lost souls, and/or Satan out of a possessed person's body and/or soul, a haunted house, a cursed object, etc. It usually involves such activities as invoking God, Jesus, angels, saints, pouring holy water on the patient, praying, sacrifices and amulets, fasting either by the clergy or by the patient; it is generally performed by a member of the clergy. (See Mark 16:17; Acts 19:13.)

faith: Confidence or trust in a person or thing; belief that is not based on physical proof; belief in God or in the doctrines or teachings of religion; belief in anything, usually God or in the doctrines or teachings of religion as a code of ethics, standards of merit, and so on. (See Hebrews 10:23, 38, 11; James 1:6.)

familiar spirit: A spirit or demon that is conjured and insecurely controlled, usually associated with the uses of witchcraft and similar powers. (See Acts 16:16–18.)

fasting: Abstaining from something like food, liquids, or sexual intercourse. (See Nehemiah 9:1–3; Matthew 6:16–18; Mark 9:13–29; 1 Corinthians 7:4–5.)

fear: A distressing emotion aroused by impending danger, evil, pain, etc., whether the threat is real or imagined; the feeling or condition of being afraid; to expect with alarm; to have reverential awe of, especially toward God. (See Exodus 14:13; Psalm 5:7; 27:1; Proverbs 1:7; Romans 8:15; Hebrews 13:6; 2 Timothy 1:7.)

fetters: Chains or shackles placed on the feet; anything that confines or restrains; something that serves to restrict or constrict the freedom of. (See Judges 16:21; 2 Chronicles 33:11; Psalm 2:3; 149:8; Mark 5:4.)

fight: To take part in combat; to contend with struggle; to try to prevent or oppose. (See 2 Chronicles 20:17; 1 Timothy 6:12.)

five names of crowns: The Crown of Life (Martyr's Crown), the Crown of Glory (Shepherd's Crown), the Crown of Rejoicing (Soul-Winner's Crown), the Crown of Righteousness, the Crown Incorruptible (Victor's Crown).

a. The Crown of Life or Martyr's Crown: Given to those who *"endure temptation."* Given to those who have been tested almost beyond human endurance. This crown is mentioned twice in Scripture. (See James 1:12; Revelation 2:10.)

b. The Crown of Glory or Shepherd's Crown: Given by the Chief Shepherd when He shall appear. (See 1 Peter 5:2–4.)

c. The Crown of Rejoicing or Soul-Winner's Crown: Given to those who have turned many to righteousness. Those brought to Jesus by us will be our "Crown of Rejoicing" at His coming. (See 1 Thessalonians 2:19.)

d. The Crown of Righteousness: Those who *"love His appearing"* will be getting ready along the journey of life to qualify for this crown. The blood of Jesus saves, yet how we live in accordance with God's holiness will determine if we receive this crown. This crown for those who "love His appearing" will be given *"on that day"*—the day of His appearing. (See 2 Timothy 4:8).

e.   The Crown Incorruptible (Victor's Crown): "Incorruptible" means there will be no devastation or tarnishing of this crown. This is the "Victor's Crown" and is for those who "discipline their bodies"—who do not yield to their fleshly lusts, nor permit themselves to be diverted from the Master's vineyard. (See 1 Corinthians 9:25–27).

fortress: A fortified place, especially a large, permanent military stronghold that often includes a town; any place of exceptional security; a stronghold or structure used to defend against attack; a fortified defensive structure. (See 2 Samuel 5:9–10.)

foothold: A place where a person may stand or walk securely; a secure position, especially a firm basis for further progress or development. (See Ephesians 4:27.)

fortune-teller: A person who claims the ability to predict the future. (See Isaiah 2:6; Micah 5:12.)

fruits of the Spirit: Love, joy, peace, patience, kindness, goodness, faithfulness, gentleness, self-control; the signs that the Holy Spirit dwells inside of someone. (See Galatians 5:19–22.)

generational curse: A family's history of generating or begetting or passing down defeat and destruction rather than blessings. (See Luke 11:46–52.)

gifts of the Spirit: Listed as word of wisdom, word of knowledge, gifts of healing, miraculous powers, prophecy, distinguishing between spirits, diverse kinds of tongues, interpretation of tongues. All these are the work of one and the same Spirit, and He gives them to each believer, as He determines. These gifts were supernaturally bestowed on the early Christians, each having his own proper gift or gifts for the edification and building up of the body of Christ. These were the result of the extraordinary operation of the Spirit, as on the day of Pentecost. Sometimes these gifts were communicated and transferred through the laying on of the hands of the apostles.

(See Mark 16:17–18; Acts 8:17, 19:6; 1 Corinthians 12:1–30; 14:1; 1 Timothy 4:14.)

good fight of faith: To engage in an advantageous conflict; satisfactory for the purpose of battle or a single combat; attempt to defend oneself against or to subdue, defeat, or destroy an adversary of confidence or trust in a person or thing. (See 1 Corinthians 9:26; Ephesians 6:11–17; 1 Timothy 6:12; 2 Timothy 2:3–5.)

heaven: Chiefly, the upper part of the universe in contradistinction to the earth; the region in which sun, moon, and stars are placed; it is stretched out as a curtain and is founded upon the mountains as on pillars sunk into the waters of the earth. It is the dwelling place of God, from which He looks down upon all the inhabitants of the earth, though the heavens and heaven's heaven do not contain Him. It is also the dwelling place of the angels. From heaven comes the rain, the hail, and the lightning; the God of Israel is eminently the God of heaven— the *"possessor of heaven and earth"*—of the world above and the world below. (See Genesis 1:1; 8:2; 14:19; 17; 19:24; 21:17; 22:11; 24:3; 28:12; Exodus 9:23; Deuteronomy 11:11; 2 Samuel 22:8; 1 Kings 8:27; Job 38:37; Psalm 11:4; 33:13–14; Proverbs 8:7–29; Isaiah 50:22; 56:1.)

hell: A place or state in which the souls of the unsaved will suffer the consequences of sin; an eternal place, those damned to hell are without hope. (See Psalm 16:10; Luke 16:19–31; Acts 2:27; Ephesians 4:8–10; Revelation 1:8, 9:1–21.)

high thing: Advanced in complexity, development, or elaboration. (See 2 Corinthians 10:5.)

holiness: The state of being devoted or dedicated to a divine character or nature; consecrated; godlike; characteristic of or befitting the Supreme Being; sanctification; set apart to a scared purpose or for religious use; a title of the Pope, formerly used also of other high ecclesiastics. (See 1 Thessalonians 4:7; 1 Timothy 2:15; Titus 2:3; Hebrews 12:14.)

humility: The state of being courteously respectful; meek; forbearing; yielding; submissive or compliant; to reduce or lower; self-abasement. (See Proverbs 22:4; Philippians 4:12; 1 Peter 5:5.)

hypnosis: An artificially induced trance state resembling sleep, characterized by heightened susceptibility to suggestion. (See Deuteronomy 18:11; Isaiah 19:3.)

infirmity: A bodily ailment or weakness, especially one brought on by old age; frailty; feebleness; a condition or disease-producing weakness; a failure or defect in a person's character. (See Leviticus 12:2; Luke 13:10–13; John 5:4–6; Romans 6:18–20.)

intercession: An act or instance of interceding; an interposing or pleading on behalf of another person; a prayer to God on behalf of another; entreaty in favor of another, especially a prayer or petition to God in behalf of another; mediation in a dispute. (See Genesis 18:16–33; Psalm 20; Isaiah 53:12; 1 Timothy 2:1.)

jealousy: An emotion typically referring to the negative thoughts and feelings of insecurity, fear, and anxiety over an anticipated loss of something that the person values, such as a relationship, friendship, or love. Jealousy often consists of a combination of emotions such as anger, sadness, and disgust. Often a protective reaction to a perceived threat to a valued relationship, arising from a situation in which the partner's involvement with an activity and/or another person is contrary to the jealous person's definition of their relationship. (See Proverbs 6:33–35; Song of Solomon 8:6; 1 Corinthians 10:21–23.)

judgment: The ability to make a decision or form an opinion objectively, authoritatively, and wisely, especially in matters affecting action; good sense; discretion. (See Exodus 12:12; Psalm 37:30, 89:14; Proverbs 21:3.)

kingdom: The administration of God; ranking, distinguishing characteristics of a king; sovereign authority and rule; dominion; monarchy; any territory or country subject to a king or queen; distinguished by leading or ruling characteristics; a principal division; a department, such as the mineral kingdom. (See Matthew 4:17.)

kingdom of God: The spiritual domain over which God is sovereign. According to Jesus, the kingdom of God is within (or among) people, is approached through understanding, and entered through acceptance like a child, spiritual rebirth, and doing the will of God.

It is a kingdom that will be inherited by the righteous and is not the only kingdom. (See Daniel 2:44; 7:18, 27; Matthew 3:2; Luke 13:20; 17:20; 1 Corinthians 4:20.)

kingdom of Satan: The devil rules this world and wages war against the kingdom of God. (See Job 1:9; Matthew 12:26; Mark 3:24; Luke 11:18.)

legion of demons: Multitude of disembodied spirits; harmful habits or distractions that inhabit or visit the believer to block them from revelation, liberty, peace, and prosperity. (See Mark 5:1, 9; Luke 8:31.)

liar: A person or spiritual being who deliberately tells false statements with the intention to deceive; someone who is influenced to mislead by an evil or demonic spirit. (See 1 John 2:22.)

lie: A false statement made with deliberate intent to deceive; an intentional untruth; a falsehood; something intended or serving to convey a false impression. (See Genesis 3:4; 2 Chronicles 18:22; Proverbs 6:16–19; John 8:44.)

linked: A term sometimes used to indicate a connection between a person and a demon. For example, there may be linkage to a principality demon in one's hometown. This term is similar to bondage. (See Genesis 3:15; Matthew 9:32–33.)

loose: To free or release from attachment; to free from anything that binds or restrains; unfetter. (See Psalm 102:19–21; 116:15–17; 146:6–8; Isaiah 58:5–7; Daniel 3:24–26; Matthew 16:18–20; Mark 7:34–36; Luke 13:11–13; Acts 16:25–27.)

Lucifer: The archangel cast from heaven for leading the revolt of the angels; originally known as the bearer of light or morning star; called *Satan* after being cast out of heaven. (See Isaiah 14:12–17; Ezekiel 28:12–19; Luke 10:18; Revelation 2:5.)

mansions in heaven: God's spiritual house in which are many abiding places. (See Ephesians 2:19–22; Hebrews 3:5–6; 1 Peter 2:5; 1 John 14:2; Revelation 3:12.)

mind: The element, part, substance, or process that reasons, thinks, feels, wills, perceives, judges, etc. in a human or other conscious being; a way of thinking or understanding; the organized conscious and unconscious adaptive mental activity of an organism. (See Ephesians 4:23; Philippians 2:5.)

mind-altering drugs: Drug use often draws demons, because the drugs can open the mind to supernatural intrusions. The Holy Spirit is too much a gentleman to fill you while you are under the influence of drugs. The same can't be said for demons. They delight in finding a person on a drug trip and being right there when that person comes down from the chemical high. (See 1 Thessalonians 5:5–8; Revelation 9:21; 18:23.)

names of angels:

  a.   Angel of the Lord (sometimes referring to Jesus: *Logos*, the Word): Genesis 16:7–14; 22:11–18; 31:11–13; 32:23–26; John 1:1–3.

  b.   Lucifer: Isaiah 14:9–19; Ezekiel 28:11–19.

  c.   Michael: Jude 1:9; Revelation 12:7.

  d.   Gabriel: Daniel 8:15–17; 9:21; Matthew 1:18–21; Luke 1:19, 26–28.

  e.   Cherubim: Genesis 3:24.

  f.   Seraphim: Isaiah 6:1–6.

nightmare: A terrifying dream in which the dreamer experiences feelings of helplessness, extreme anxiety, sorrow, etc.; formerly a monster or evil spirit believed to oppress persons during sleep. (See Psalm 55:5; 91:5–6.)

occult: Of or pertaining to magic, astrology, or any system claiming use or knowledge of secret or supernatural powers or agencies. (See Exodus 7:11; 8:7, 9:11.)

oppression: In the New Testament Greek, this refers to a person having a host of fallen angels exercised against a person; it involves a serious level of demonization. (See Ecclesiastes 4:1–8; Acts 10:38.)

ordinance: An authoritative rule or law; a decree or command; a public injunction or regulation: e.g., a city ordinance against excessive horn-blowing; something believed to have been ordained, as by a deity or destiny; ecclesiastical: an established rite or ceremony; a sacrament; the communion. (See Colossians 2:20.)

paradise: A place of extreme perfection or a connecting location between life and immortality; supernatural state of being during a connection with God characterized by revelation, peace, and wisdom. (See Luke 23:43; 2 Corinthians 12:4; Revelation 2:7.)

pastor: A shepherd or overseer of a local assembly; watchmen of spiritual matters relating to people's souls. (See Ephesians 4:11; Acts 20:38.)

petition: A request made for something desired, especially a respectful or humble request, as to a superior or to one in authority; a supplication or prayer: a request for aid; a prayer to God for courage and strength. (See 1 Chronicles 16:4; Ezra 8:23; Esther 5:8; 7:2, 3; 9:12.)

plead the blood of Jesus: To declare with positivity and claim the benefits of the blood (life) of Jesus in defense or justification, or to stand in His forgiveness, protection, or provision. (See Exodus 12; John 1:29; Ephesians 2:13; Hebrews 10:19; 1 Peter 1:2; 1 John 1:7; Revelation 12:11.)

possession, demonic: Domination by an evil spirit; a psychological or spiritual state in which an individual's normal personality is replaced by another's. (See Matthew 8:16, 27–29; 9:31–33; Mark 5:15; Luke 8:36.)

poverty: The state or condition of having little or no money, goods, or means of support; the condition of being poor; indigence; deficiency of necessary or desirable ingredients, qualities, etc.; scantiness; insufficiency. (See 1 Samuel 2:7; Proverbs 13:18; 20:13; Revelation 2:9.)

power: A particular ability, capability, or skill; strength, force, or might; the authority or ability to control others. (See Romans 8:38–39; Ephesians 6:12; Colossians 2:15.)

praise: The act of expressing approval or admiration; commendation; laudation; the offering of grateful homage in words or song, as an act of worship or a hymn of praise to God; the state of being approved or admired. (See Acts 16:25–34.)

prayer: To converse with God; the intercourse of the soul with God, not in contemplation or meditation, but in direct address to him. Prayer may be oral or mental, occasional or constant, exclamatory or formal. It is a beseeching of the Lord; pouring out the soul before God; praying and crying to heaven; seeking God and making supplication; drawing near to God; bowing the knee. (See Exodus 32:11; 1 Samuel 1:15; 2 Chronicles 32:20; Job 8:5; Psalm 73:28; Ephesians 3:14.)

pride: A high or misguided opinion of one's own dignity, importance, merit, or superiority, whether as cherished in the mind or as displayed in bearing, conduct, conceit, self-esteem, egotism, vanity, vainglory, etc. (See Ezekiel 28; Proverbs 16:18.)

prince of darkness: One of the gods of the Arvites who colonized part of Samaria after the deportation of Israel by Shalmaneser; a prince, a male ruler of a principality; a wicked entity that spreads darkness, i.e., absence of light. (See 2 Kings 17:31.)

principalities: The territory or jurisdiction ruled by a prince. A particular area marked by rules and a single train of thought. (See Romans 8:38; Ephesians 3:10; Colossians 1:16.)

prophecy: The utterance by or as if by divine inspiration. (See 1 Corinthians 14:13; 2 Peter 1:21; 2:10.)

prophet: One who is in tune with God in such a way that the Holy Spirit shares unannounced truths; one who speaks for God to man. (See Numbers 11:17–29; 1 Samuel 9:9.)

purpose: An object, goal, or desired accomplishment to be reached. The end of a directed course that has been set, with measured results. To expect or design an end or accomplishment. (See Matthew 26:8.)

rank: An establishment of positions to maintain and monitor order within a system. (See Colossians 1:16.)

rebellion: Resistance to or defiance of any authority, control, or tradition. (See 1 Samuel 15:23.)

rebuke: To express sharp, stern disapproval of; reprove; reprimand. (See Matthew 17:14–21.)

recompense: Restitution or payback; a squaring away; an equal deserved substitution or compensation for services or loss; a giving in place of a loss or suffering; to pay back a perceived earned or deserved thing; an equivalent returned for anything done, suffered, or given; compensation; requital; suitable return. (See Luke 6:35.)

refuge: A shelter or protection from danger, trouble, etc.; for example, to take refuge from a storm; a place of shelter, protection, or safety; anything to which one has recourse for aid, relief, or escape; a source of help or comfort in times of trouble. (See Deuteronomy 33:27–28; 2 Samuel 22:2–4; Psalm 57:1.)

regeneration: Spiritual or moral revival or rebirth. (See Psalm 80:18; 85:6; Isaiah 57:15; Hosea 6:2; Titus 3:4–7.)

render: To give an account for, based on judged value; to return or pay back; to restore; to inflict, as a retribution; to requite. (See Matthew 6:18.)

repent: To feel remorse or self-reproach for what one has done or failed to do; to be contrite. (See Genesis 6:6; Numbers 23:19; Judges 2:18; Matthew 3:1–3; Mark 1:14–16.)

reprobate: Existing in a state of unbelief, persistent refusal to accept truth despite overwhelming evidence; to condemn strongly as unworthy, unacceptable, or evil; to foreordain to damnation. (See Romans 1:28; 2 Timothy 3:8; Titus 1:16.)

resist: To withstand, strive against, or oppose; to withstand the action or effect of; to refrain or abstain from, especially with difficulty or reluctance. (See Numbers 31:23; 2 Timothy 3:8; James 4:7.)

resurrection: The act of rising from the dead; the rising of Christ after His death and burial; the rising of the dead on Judgment Day. (See Matthew 22:31; 27:52–54; John 11:23–25.)

right relationship (with God): In conformity with fact, reason, truth, or some standard or principle; that which is in accord with fact, reason, propriety, the way of thinking that conforms to fact or truth, in a connection, association, or involvement with another or others. (See Deuteronomy 11:22–25; Psalm 91; Philippians 2:12.)

rulers of the darkness: Legal powers and/or authorities with jurisdiction and authorization to exercise power devoid of God's light; entities that choose not to subscribe to God's light or which turn their back on God's light. (See Ephesians 6:12.)

salvation: The act of saving or protecting from harm, risk, loss, destruction, etc.; the state of being saved or protected from harm or risk; a source, cause, or means of being saved or protected from harm, risk, etc.; deliverance from the power and penalty of sin; redemption. (See Acts 2; Romans 10:9–10.)

sanctification: To reserve for sacred use; consecrate. (See 1 Peter 1:2; 1 Corinthians 1:30; 1 Thessalonians 4:3–4; 2 Thessalonians 2:13.)

Satan: The chief evil spirit; the great adversary of humanity; often identified with the leader of the fallen angels. (See Job 1:6–12; 2:1–7; Ezekiel 28:12–19.)

Satanic trinity (Triumvirate): The Dragon, the Beast, and the False Prophet are the three persons or postures of Satan that are in direct opposition to the Godhead (Trinity). (See Daniel 7; Mark 2:5–6; John 10:33; Revelation 13:11–18; 14:9–10, 16.)

a.   The Dragon (Anti-God) is the Father of Lies.

b.   The Beast (Anti-Christ) is the Son of Perdition.

c.   The False Prophet (Anti-Spirit) is the False Spirit.

saved: To be rescued from harm, danger, or loss, brought to a safe position. (See 1 Corinthians 15:1–4.)

séance: A meeting in which a spiritualist attempts to communicate with the spirits of the dead, a practice forbidden in the Scriptures. (See Deuteronomy 18:10; Acts 16:16.)

secret place: Kept from the knowledge of any but the initiated or privileged: e.g., a secret password; designed or working to escape notice, knowledge, or observation; secluded, sheltered, or withdrawn: e.g., a secret hiding place; someplace that has been or is kept secret, hidden, or concealed; someplace that remains beyond understanding or explanation; a mystery. (See Psalm 91.)

seducing spirits: Evil spirits that persuade, entice, and deceive; spirits that draw one away from proper conduct. (See 2 Corinthians 11:14–15; 1 Timothy 4:1; 1 John 4:1; Revelation 16:14.)

seraphim: Angelic beings associated with fire, depicted as having six wings; heavenly attendants to the throne of God. (See Isaiah 6:1–7; Revelation 4:8–9.)

shield of faith: Confidence or trust in a person or thing for protection; belief in anything, usually God or in the doctrines or teachings of religion as a code of ethics, standards of merit, etc. as a protective device or structure. (See Ephesians 6:16.)

sin: Transgression of divine law: e.g., the sin of Adam; any act regarded as a transgression, especially a willful or deliberate violation of some religious or moral principle; any reprehensible or regrettable action, behavior, lapse, etc.; great fault or offense: e.g., "It's a sin to waste time"; to commit a sinful act; to offend against a principle, standard, etc. (See Romans 3:23–26; 6:16; 7; 8:1–9; Galatians 5.)

slothful: To be sluggardly; indolent; lazy; habitually inactive or lazy. (See Proverbs 6:6; 13:4.)

snare: Anything serving to entrap or entangle unawares; to catch or involve by trickery or wile. (See Exodus 34:12; Psalm 38:12; 64:5; 119:110; Proverbs 6:2.)

spirit: The principle of conscious life; the vital principle in humans, animating the body or mediating between body and soul; the soul regarded as separating from the body at death; conscious, immaterial being, as opposed to matter; a supernatural, immaterial being, especially one inhabiting a place, object, etc., or having a particular character; an angel or demon; an attitude or principle that inspires, animates, or pervades thought, feeling or action; a divine, inspiring, or animating being or influence (see Numbers 11:25; Isaiah 32:15); the third person of the Trinity, the Holy Spirit; the soul or heart as the seat of feelings or sentiments, or as prompting to action; the general meaning or intent of a statement, document, etc.; a special attitude or frame of mind. (See John 14:17; 16:13.)

spell: Any dominating or irresistible influence; fascination; a spoken word or form of words held to have magic power. (See Job 38:31.)

sober: Marked by seriousness; free from excess, extravagance, or exaggeration; showing self-control; sane or rational. (See 1 Thessalonians 5:5–8.)

sorcery: The art, practices, or spells of a person believed to exercise supernatural powers through the aid of evil spirits; the mysterious ability to influence, fascinate, charm, and captivate; the use of power gained from the assistance or control of evil spirits, especially for foreseeing or foretelling future events or discovering hidden knowledge. (See Exodus 7:11, 22; Acts 8:9.)

soul: The principle of life, feeling, thought, and action in humans, regarded as a distinct entity separate from the body and commonly held to be separable in existence from the body; the spiritual part of humans as distinct from the physical part; the spiritual part of humans regarded in its moral aspect, or as believed to survive death and be subject to happiness or misery in a life to come; the disembodied spirit of a deceased person; the divine source of all identity and individuality; shared ethnic awareness and pride among black people, especially black Americans. (See Proverbs 11:30.)

standard: A rule or principle that is used as a basis for judgment; an authorized exemplar of a unit of weight or measure; an upright support; a flag or banner indicating the presence of a sovereign official; an emblematic figure or other object raised on a pole to indicate the rallying point of an army, fleet, etc. (See Numbers 2:17; 10:13–14; Isaiah 49:22; 59:19; 62:10.)

strife: Discord or conflict. (See Proverbs 15:18; 26:30; 2 Timothy 2:23; James 3:16.)

stronghold: A defensive spiritual fortress behind which one hides and is protected from the enemy; a fortress or fortified place; a place of security or survival; a place dominated by a particular group or marked by a particular characteristic; an area dominated or occupied by a special group or distinguished by a special quality. (See Numbers 13:19; Judges 6:2; 9:46, 49; 1 Samuel 22:4–5; 23:14, 29; 24:22; 2 Samuel 5:7, 9, 17; 22:3; 24:7; 2 Kings 8:12; 1 Chronicles 11:5, 7, 16; 9:12.)

strongman: The man or spirit who is in charge or who has total authority; the most powerful or influential person in an organization, business, or environment by reason of skill in the formulation and execution of plans, work, etc. (See 1 Samuel 14:52; Mark 3:27; Luke 11:21–22.)

strong tower: A building or structure high in proportion to its lateral dimensions, either isolated or forming part of a building; such a structure used as or intended for a stronghold or fortress; any of various fully enclosed fireproof housings for vertical communications, such as staircases, between the stories of a building; a tall, movable structure used in ancient and medieval warfare in storming a fortified place. (See Psalm 61:2–3; Proverbs 18:10.)

subtle: Difficult to perceive or understand; mysterious; requiring mental acuteness, penetration, or discernment; skillful, clever, or ingenious. (See Genesis 3:1; 2 Corinthians 11:3.)

superstition: A belief or notion, not based on reason or knowledge, typically in the ominous significance of a particular thing, circumstance, occurrence, proceeding, or the like. (See 1 Timothy 4:7.)

sword: A long, edged piece of metal, used in many civilizations throughout the world, primarily as a cutting or thrusting weapon and occasionally for clubbing; a weapon having various forms but consisting typically of a long, straight, or slightly curved blade, sharp-edged on one or both sides, with one end pointed and the other fixed in a hilt or handle; this weapon as a symbol of military power, punitive justice, or authority; war, combat, slaughter, or violence through military force or aggression. (See Genesis 3:24; 34:36; Judges 7:18;

2 Samuel 2:26; Psalm 22:20; 57:4; Proverbs 5:4; Isaiah 2:4; Jeremiah 47:8; Amos 7:11; Micah 4:3; Matthew 10:34; 26:51–53; Luke 2:35; Romans 8:35; 13:4; Ephesians 6:17; Hebrews 4:12; Revelation 1:16; 19:15.)

sword of the spirit: A powerful weapon of spiritual warfare. This sword is formed by speaking God's Word. In discussing the sword of the Spirit, it is helpful to first examine the meaning of the Greek words *logos* and *rhema*, which are often used for the Word of God. *Logos* is often used to identify the written Scriptures in the Bible. *Rhema* is more often used of the spoken word of God. (See Ephesians 6:17; Hebrews 4:12.)

tempt: To entice or allure to do something often regarded as unwise, wrong, or immoral; to attract, appeal strongly to, or invite; to render strongly disposed to do something; to put someone to the test in a venturesome way; provoke: e.g., to tempt one's fate; to try or test. (See Matthew 26:40–41; Mark 14:38; Luke 14:13; 22:40–46; 1 Corinthians 10:6–13; James 1:12.)

testimony: An undeniable experience with God in the past that sustains one for present or future difficulties; evidence in support of a fact or statement; proof. (See Revelation 11:7; 12:11.)

throne: The official chair or seat upon which a monarch is seated on state or ceremonial occasions; depicted as God's representation on earth; Jesus promised His apostles that they would sit upon "twelve thrones," judging the twelve tribes of Israel. (See 1 Kings 10:18; Psalm 122:5; Isaiah 14:8–10; Ezekiel 26:15–17; Daniel 7:9; Matthew 19:28; 25:31; Luke 22:30; Colossians 1:16; Revelation 4:2–11; 5:5–6; 7:10–11, 15, 17; 14:3; 20:4; 22:1.)

tongue: A dialect; speech, often incomprehensible, typically uttered during moments of religious ecstasy: e.g., speaking in tongues, a form of glossolalia in which a person experiencing utters incomprehensible sounds that the speaker believes are a language spoken through him or her by a deity; gift of tongues. (See Joel 2:28; Acts 2:1–47; 1 Corinthians 12; 14:2–19, 26.)

Trinity (Godhead): The Father, Son, and Holy Spirit are the three persons or postures of God. (See Isaiah 48:16; Matthew 3:16–17; 28:18–20; Luke 3:21–22; John 14:26; 16:13–15; 2 Corinthians 13:14; Galatians 4:6; Ephesians 2:18; 4:4–6; 5:18–20; 1 Peter 1:2; 1 John 5:7.)

triumph: The act, fact, or condition of being victorious; a significant success or noteworthy achievement. (See Exodus 15:1, 21; 1 Samuel 17:50; Psalm 25:2; 47:1; 92:4; 106:47; 2 Corinthians 2:14.)

truth: The actual state of a matter; reality; an indisputable fact, proposition, principle or the like; sincerity in action, character, and utterance. (See Genesis 32:10; Exodus 18:21; Psalm 15:2; 25:5; Proverbs 3:3; 12:17; 16:6; Luke 9:27; John 4:23.)

unbelief: The state or quality of not believing; incredulity or skepticism, especially in matters of doctrine or religious faith. (See Matthew 17:19–20; Mark 9:23; Hebrews 11.)

vain imagination: The faculty of imagining or forming mental images or concepts of what is not actually present to the senses; the action or process of forming such images or concepts. (See Romans 1:21; 2 Corinthians 10:5.)

vibration: A supernatural emanation, good or evil, that is sensed by or revealed to those attuned or in harmony with the occult or with God; a general emotional feeling derived from another person, place, situation, etc.; a characteristic emanation, aura, or spirit that infuses or vitalizes someone or something and that can be instinctively sensed or experienced; a distinctive, usually emotional, atmosphere capable of being sensed; perception. (See Judges 6:22; Ecclesiastes 1:17; Matthew 22:18; Mark 2:8; Luke 1:22; 5:22; 20:23.)

victory: A success or triumph over an enemy in battle or war; the ultimate and decisive superiority in any battle or contest; a successful or superior position achieved against any opponent, difficulty, etc.; a successful outcome to a struggle; the decisive defeat of an opponent in a contest of any kind; the overcoming of an enemy or antagonist. (See 2 Samuel 23:10, 12; Isaiah 25:8; 1 Corinthians 15:53–55, 57.)

vigilant: Keenly watchful to detect danger; ever awake and alert. (See 1 Timothy 3:1–3; 1 Peter 5:8.)

vision: The act or power of sensing with the eyes; sight; the act or power of anticipating that which will or may come to be; an experience in which a personage, thing, or event appears vividly or credibly to the mind, although not actually present, often under the influence of a divine force or other agency; something seen or otherwise perceived during such an experience; a vivid, imaginative conception or anticipation; something seen; an object of sight. (See Proverbs 29:18; Joel 2:28.)

warfare: Armed conflict between enemies; struggle; discord. (See 2 Corinthians 10:4.)

warring in the spirit: Armed fighting in the spiritual realm; fighting as a science, profession, activity, or art; to be in conflict or in a state of strong opposition; a state of open, armed, often prolonged conflict carried on between oneself and celestial powers, often in conflict with God. (See Ephesians 6:12.)

weapons: Instruments or devices used for offense or defense; a means employed to contend with another. (See John 18:3; 2 Corinthians 10:4.)

wealth: A great quantity or store of money, valuable possessions, property, or other riches; all things that have a monetary or exchange value; anything that has utility and is capable of being appropriated or exchanged; rich or valuable contents or produce; the state of being rich; prosperity; affluence. (See Deuteronomy 8:18; Psalm 49:6–7; Proverbs 10:15; 13:11, 22; 19:4; Ecclesiastes 5:19; 6:2; Acts 19:25.)

weight: The relative importance or authority given something; measurable influence, especially on others; overpowering force; a force that results from the action of gravity on matter. (See Proverbs 11:1; 16:11; Matthew 23:23; 2 Corinthians 4:17; Hebrews 12:1.)

wile: A trick or behavior meant to fool, trap, or entice; a device; artful, deceitfully cunning behavior. (See Numbers 25:18; Ephesians 6:11.)

witch: A person who professes the practice of black magic; a believer or follower of Wicca; a woman considered to be spiteful or overbearing; a woman who works to cast a spell. (See Deuteronomy 18:10.)

witchcraft: The art or practices of a witch; sorcery; magic; magical influence; producing illusions through the use of deceptive devices; domination; manipulation; intimidation. (See 1 Samuel 15:23; 2 Chronicles 33:6; Galatians 5:20.)

Word of God: A manifestation of the mind and will of God; e.g., the Scriptures are the written Word of God; the infallible authority by which God directs and governs all. (See Joshua 1:13; Psalm 119:114; Isaiah 38:4–5; Luke 8:11, 21, 28; John 1:1; 2 Timothy 2:9.)

works: Deeds, activities, callings, or missions. (See Matthew 11:2; Mark 13:34; 1 Timothy 2:10.)

works of darkness: Actions that are evil or morally bad in principle or practice; wickedness; mischievous or playfully malicious; actions done out of spite. (See Romans 13:11–14; Ephesians 5:11.)

works (deeds) of the flesh: Listed in Galatians 5:19–21:

    a.   Adultery: To have unlawful intercourse with another's wife. (See Exodus 20:14; Leviticus 20:10; Romans 13:9.)

    b.   Fornication: Illicit sexual intercourse, including homosexuality, bestiality, harlotry, or any sexual activity outside of marriage. (See Matthew 19:9; 1 Corinthians 6:18.)

    c.   Uncleanness: Used in a moral sense, the impurity of lustful, luxurious, profligate living, with impure motives. (See Matthew 5:8; Philippians 4:8.)

    d.   Lasciviousness: Unbridled lust, excess, licentiousness, wantonness, outrageousness, shamelessness, or insolence. (See Matthew 5:27–30; Mark 7:20–23.)

    e.   Idolatry: The worship of false gods. (See Exodus 20:2–6; Deuteronomy 5:6–9; 7:23–26; 2 Kings 21:11–15; 1 Corinthians 10:14.)

f. Witchcraft: Sorcery, magical arts, often found in connection with idolatry and fostered by it. (See Isaiah 8:19–20; Acts 13:6–12.)

g. Hatred: Enmity or hostility. (See Titus 3:3; 1 John 3:15.)

h. Variance: Contention, strife, or wrangling. (See 1 Corinthians 3:3; Titus 3:9; Jude 1:3.)

i. Emulations: Envious and contentious rivalry or jealousy. (See Romans 13:13; James 3:16.)

j. Wrath: Passion, angry, heat, or anger, typically boiling up and soon subsiding again. (See Ephesians 4:31–32; Colossians 3:8.)

k. Strife: A desire to put one's self forward; a partisan and fractious spirit. (See Philippians 2:3.)

l. Seditions: Dissensions or divisions; divisive behavior. (See 1 Corinthians 1:10; Romans 16:17–18.)

m. Heresies: Dissensions arising from diversity of opinions and aims. False teachers bear this trait. (See 2 Peter 2:1–3.) The Bible is clear that unity cannot exist among diverse beliefs. (See Amos 3:3; Philippians 3:16; 2 Thessalonians 2:15; 2 John 1:9–11.)

n. Envy: To harbor envy or jealousy. Pilate realized Jesus was set to be killed because of this motivation. (See Matthew 27:13–18; Mark 15:10.) We should lay aside envy and simply trust the Word of God. (See 1 Peter 2:1–2.)

o. Murder: Greek *phonos*, to murder or slaughter. As with other sins, it is from the heart that this sin is born. (See Matthew 15:19.) Unless there is repentance, a murderer can know that heaven will not be their home. (See Revelation 21:8.) God's Word clearly states when life begins (see Job 3:3; Jeremiah 1:5; Luke 1:40–41), which shows why abortion is such a serious offense.

p.   Drunkenness: Intoxication, usually because of alcohol; inebriation, a condition that is not wise and which can lead to being separated from other believers. (See Proverbs 20:1; 1 Corinthians 5:9–11.)

worship: Reverence offered to a divine being or supernatural power; an act of expressing such reverence; a form of religious practice with its creed and ritual; extravagant respect or admiration for or devotion to an object of esteem. (See Joshua 5:14–15; Nehemiah 9:6; Psalm 45:11, 17; 72:15; 145:18; Daniel 3:8–30; Matthew 2:2, 11; 9:18; John 4:24; 1 Corinthians 16:19; Philippians 2:9–11; Hebrews 1:6; 11:32–34.)

wrestle: To contend, as in a struggle for mastery; grapple. (See Genesis 32:24–25; Ephesians 6:12.)

yoke: A curved apparatus formerly laid on the neck of a defeated person; a frame used to bind two parts, to hold or unite them in position; a wooden bar by which two animals (such as oxen) are joined at the heads or necks for working together; a frame fitted to a person's shoulders to carry a load in two equal portions; an oppressive agency. (See Genesis 27:40; Leviticus 26:13; 1 Kings 12:4; Isaiah 9:4; 10:27; 58:6; Jeremiah 28:10–14; Lamentations 1:14; Ezekiel 34:27; Matthew 11:29–30; Acts 15:10; Galatians 5:1.)

APPENDIX A: SCRIPTURAL PRINCIPLES FOR SPIRITUAL PURITY

Overcome Through the Holy Spirit

+ Jesus was tempted in every way, just as we are, yet didn't sin. (See Hebrews 4:15.)

+ God's Spirit in you is greater than the spirit of wickedness in the world. (See 1 John 4:4.)

+ In spite of trials, be encouraged because Jesus overcame the world. (See John 16:33.)

Repent and Receive Forgiveness

+ You can be sure that your sin will be uncovered. (See Numbers 32:23.)

+ If you conceal sin, you won't prosper, so you should confess it and receive mercy. (See Proverbs 28:13.)

+ If you confess your sins, He is faithful to forgive and purify you. (See 1 John 1:9.)

Pursue Purity

+ Separate yourselves from the world and be holy, because God is holy. (See Leviticus 11:44–45.)

+ Make a covenant with your eyes not to look lustfully at members of the opposite sex. (See Job 31:1.)

- If you look lustfully at someone, you've already sinned in your heart. (See Matthew 5:28–30.)

- Don't compromise or make any provision to fulfill lustful desires. (See Romans 13:14.)

- You were washed, sanctified, and justified by the Holy Spirit. (See 1 Corinthians 6:9–11.)

- Flee sexual immorality. You are not your own; you were bought at a price. (See 1 Corinthians 6:18, 20.)

- Avoid sexual immorality, control your body, live a pure and honorable life. (See 1 Thessalonians 4:3–8.)

- Avoid any hint of sexual immorality, obscenity, or coarse jesting. (See Ephesians 5:3–4.)

- Hide God's Word in your heart, so you won't sin against Him. (See Psalm 119:11.)

- Don't be ignorant or unaware of the devil's schemes. (See 2 Corinthians 2:11.)

- Be alert and self-controlled, because the devil seeks someone to devour. (See 1 Peter 5:8.)

- God's grace helps us resist worldly passions and live with self-control. (See Titus 2:11–12.)

- Submit to God and resist the devil, and he will flee from you. (See James 4:7.)

Examine and Guard Your Heart

- Evil thoughts, including sexual immorality, come out from the heart. (See Matthew 15:19–20.)

- God searches our hearts and examines our minds. (See Jeremiah 17:10.)

- Ask God to give you a new, pure heart and make your spirit right. (See Psalm 51:10.)

- Above all else, guard your heart and mind. (See Proverbs 4:23.)

- Control Your Thoughts
- Keep your thoughts focused on God; trust Him to stay in perfect peace. (See Isaiah 26:3.)
- Don't conform to the world, but be transformed by the renewing of your mind. (See Romans 12:1–2.)
- Take every thought captive, and make it obedient to Christ. (See 2 Corinthians 10:5.)
- Think about things that are honorable, right, and pure. (See Philippians 4:8.)
- Meditate on thoughts and speak words that are acceptable to the Lord. (See Psalm 19:14.)

Choose Friends Wisely

- Walk with the wise and be wise; walk with fools and suffer harm. (See Proverbs 13:20.)
- Don't be misled; bad company corrupts good character. (See 1 Corinthians 15:33.)

Remember Your High Calling and Avoid Negative Consequences

- The Lord sees all; lack of discipline leads to deception and death. (See Proverbs 5:20–23.)
- If you play with fire, you'll get burned; adultery will be punished. (See Proverbs 6:27–29.)
- God will judge or reward every man based on his conduct. (See Jeremiah 17:10.)
- Sowing to your lower nature brings a harvest of decay and death. (See Galatians 6:7–8.)
- The wicked and sexually immoral will not inherit God's kingdom. (See 1 Corinthians 6:9–11.)
- Remember your high calling as God's child and part of His royal priesthood and holy nation. (See 1 Peter 1:13–21; 2:9–10.)

APPENDIX B: BOOKS FOR FREEDOM FROM SEXUAL TEMPTATION AND ADDICTION

Books for Men

At the Altar of Sexual Idolatry by Steve Gallagher

Breaking Free: Understanding Sexual Addiction and the Healing Power of Jesus by Russell Willingham

Every Man's Battle: Winning the War on Sexual Temptation One Victory at a Time by Stephen Arterburn and Fred Stoeker

Every Man's Battle Guide: Weapons for the War Against Sexual Temptation by Stephen Arterburn and Fred Stoeker

Every Day for Every Man: 365 Readings for Those Engaged in the Battle by Stephen Arterburn and Fred Stoeker

False Intimacy: Understanding the Struggle of Sexual Addiction by Harry Schaumburg

Healing the Wounds of Sexual Addiction by Mark Laaser and Gary Smalley

I Surrender All: Rebuilding a Marriage Broken by Pornography by Clay and Renee Crosse

L.I.F.E. Guide for Men by Mark Laaser

Manhood: Let the Truth Be Told by Tom Fortson

Men's Secret Wars by Patrick A. Means

Pure Desire: How One Man's Triumph Can Help Others Break Free from Sexual Temptation by Ted Roberts and Steve Arterburn

Pure Freedom: Breaking the Addiction to Pornography by Mike Cleveland

The Game Plan: The Men's 30-Day Strategy for Attaining Sexual Integrity by Joe Dallas

The War Within: Gaining Victory in the Battle for Sexual Purity by Robert Daniels

Think Before You Look: Avoiding the Consequences of Secret Temptation by Daniel Henderson

Secret Sins of the Heart: Freedom from the Chains of Pornography by David A. Wagner

Seven Promises of a Promise Keeper by Jack Hayford, Gary Smalley, Charles R. Swindoll, and Max Lucado

Stop Sex Addiction: Real Hope, True Freedom for Sex Addicts and Partners by Milton Magness

When Good Men Are Tempted by Bill Perkins

Books for Women

An Affair of the Mind by Laurie Hall

Every Heart Restored: A Wife's Guide to Healing in the Wake of a Husband's Sexual Sin by Stephen Arterburn and Fred and Brenda Stoeker

Every Heart Restored Workbook: A Wife's Guide to Healing in the Wake of Every Man's Battle by Stephen Arterburn and Fred and Brenda Stoeker

Every Woman's Battle: Discovering God's Plan for Sexual and Emotional Fulfillment by Shannon Ethridge and Stephen Arterburn

Hope After Betrayal: Healing When Sexual Addiction Invades Your Marriage by Meg Wilson

Living with Your Husband's Secret Wars by Marsha Means

No Stones: Women Redeemed from Sexual Addiction by Marnie C. Ferree and Mark Laaser

Prone to Wander: A Woman's Struggle with Sexual Sin and Addiction by Sabrina D. Black and LaVern A. Harlin

Prone to Wander: Prayers of Confession and Celebration by Barbara R. Duguid and Wayne Duguid Houk

Shattered Vows: Hope and Healing for Women Who Have Been Sexually Betrayed by Debra Laaser

When His Secret Sin Breaks Your Heart: Letters to Hurting Wives by Kathy Gallagher

APPENDIX C: INTERNET RESOURCES FOR OVERCOMING SEXUAL TEMPTATION

Websites

- L.I.F.E. Recovery: freedomeveryday.org
- Men of Integrity: menofintegrity.org
- Pure Online: x3pure.com
- Healing for the Soul: healingforthesoul.org
- XXXChurch: xxxchurch.com
- National Association for Christian Recovery: nacronline.com
- Focus on the Family: focusonthefamily.com

Christian Internet Filters

- Covenant Eyes: covenanteyes.com
- See No Evil Online: seenoevil.com
- Total Net Guard: afo.net
- Hedge Builders: hedge.org
- Clean Internet: cleaninter.net
- Integrity Online: integrity.com

ABOUT THE AUTHOR

Bishop George G. Bloomer is the founder and senior pastor of Bethel Family Worship Center, a multicultural congregation in Durham, North Carolina, and the Life Church in Goldsboro, North Carolina. A native of Brooklyn, New York, Bloomer overcame difficult personal challenges, as well as a destructive environment of poverty and drugs, and he uses those learning experiences as priceless tools for empowering others to excel beyond their seeming limitations.

He has appeared as a guest on several television, radio, and media outlets nationwide, including CNN's *Faces of Faith*, the Trinity Broadcasting Network (TBN), *The Harvest Show* (LeSEA Broadcasting), and *The 700 Club* (Christian Broadcasting Network). He can be seen weekly on his national television broadcast, *Spiritual Authority*.

Bloomer is the author of a number of books, including *Looking for Love*, *More of Him*, *Authority Abusers*, *Spiritual Warfare*, and the national best seller, *Witchcraft in the Pews*. He has also collaborated with Mary K. Baxter on *A Divine Revelation of Deliverance* and *A Divine Revelation of Prayer*.

He conducts many seminars dealing with relationships, finances, stress management, and spiritual warfare. In addition, he travels extensively as a conference speaker, delivering a message to liberate and impact the lives of thousands for Christ.

Bishop Bloomer has been awarded an honorary doctor of divinity degree from Christian Outreach Bible Institute.